Praise for

The Masked Sequoia

The Masked Sequoia is an extraordinary story of an orphan girl and her orphaned tree, both of whom were doomed to fail yet miraculously prevailed with courage and the sheer tenacity to seize hope and refuse to die. Not to simply survive, this story is a blueprint for what it took to find her grove and claim her place amongst the giants. You are invited to join them.
Sara White

"Honest Experience of a Brave Woman"
As someone on her own healing journey from abuse, I really loved this book because it detailed her thought processes from childhood through being a grandmother (even though I read it over a two-day period).

I was enthralled from the beginning to the end; with her story and how she tells it. She is courageously honest and truthful and reads like I was listening to an old friend over coffee.

Though not all my circumstances were the same, the impact of abuse and trauma is. I felt validated through the author's perceptions, observations, and feelings. I think you will find a kindred spirit with this author; this is a need to read for us "overcomers".
Cristina B.

Sequoia is a beautifully written and breathtaking memoir of a child of abuse, who is now a woman of abuse, striking out with her two young sons to find a life of peace. Every chapter brings you closer to the journey we share and the forest of strong, deep- rooted Sequoias we all need.
Julia Fenstermacher

I0833834

THE MASKED SEQUOIA

She is me. I am her.

Lori Leigh

The Masked Sequoia: I am her, she is me

This book is self-published in collaboration with:
Rainy Day Self-Publishing LLC
RainyDaySelfPublishing.com
Info@RainyDaySelfPublishing.com

Lori Leigh
LoriLeigh.com
Lori@LoriLeigh.com

First Publication: February 2026

For additional or bulk purchases, visit: http://amazon.com/author/lorileigh

Paperback ISBN: 979-8-218-91812-5

Printed On Demand

Dedication

To my husband, my sons, and my Tribe who have all been on this journey with me.

Contents

Trigger Warning

The author would like to warn you that this book contains discussions and mentions of:

- Childhood Abuse & Trauma
- Domestic Abuse & Trauma
- Eating Disorders
- Body Dysmorphia
- Mental Health Challenges
- Suicidal Ideation & Suicide Attempts
- Grief & Loss

These topics may be triggering for some readers, so please read at your own risk.

If you need help, a list of resources is located on Page 111.

Foreword

Looking back on the last ten plus years that I've known Lori, I see her in almost every season of my life; the good and the bad. Through the joys and pains, the growth, the healing, and so many shared memories that I can't even count them all!

What started as a friendship quickly grew into so many more titles. I truly can't name them all, but here's a few: one of my besties, my sister-in-Christ, my road-trip buddy, my partner-in-crime, my roommate at times, my shoulder to cry on, my caregiving client, my fellow author, and most recently, my business partner. She isn't just a friend. All these titles combine to show she's part of my soul family, and I am grateful to God for blessing my life with her.

Since I've known Lori, we've faced growing pains, just like any other friendship. But I've also had a front row seat to watch and support Lori as she's had to face and take on many more struggles; more than most people could even imagine or comprehend. I've seen the ups and downs of her chronic illnesses, the days when simply getting out of bed was a chore, when her mental health was overloading her mind and she was shying away from a quick side hug from men at church, and the moments when her stubbornness was brighter than her pain.

As we got to know each other more, I learned about the dark clouds that hung over Lori from her painful divorces and the terrible abuse she'd had in her childhood and in her second marriage. I've watched her battle those demons, with the help of her tribe, what she calls us friends and family, and we are not only happy to be in the trenches with her, but we are so monumentally proud of her strength and determination to break the hold her past had on her, so she could blossom into the woman we know today.

Now, our story isn't one-sided. She stood beside me through some of my hardest moments, too: losing my parents, navigating grief as an only child, and finding my way after leaving the only place I had ever truly called home. She has been steady, compassionate, and present in a way that only someone who understands suffering and grace can be.

That's why this book is so powerful. Her journey is not just about survival. It's about transformation. She has taken every painful piece of her past and shaped it into wisdom, hope, and resilience. She's chosen healing even when it meant facing wounds that ran deep. She's reclaimed herself, piece by piece, with courage that continues to inspire me.

The Masked Sequoia dives deep into her journey and offers an honest, raw, and bold look into her life. Her story reminds us that healing is possible, that no one is beyond restoration, and that even the hardest paths can lead to a life filled with purpose, hope, and light.

You'll also learn from this book that she wasn't given long to live in the mid- to late-2000s. Thankfully her doctors were wrong! If they had been, I would never have met her in 2015, so I look at her presence in my life as a gift.

I'm genuinely honored that she calls me family, and I am endlessly proud of the woman she has become and of the voice she now shares with the world.

May these pages give you the same courage, comfort, and hope she has given me.

EJ Frederiksen
February 2026

Lori (left) and EJ (right)
Hoover Dam - October 2025

Author's Note

Greetings, as we begin this journey together. I want to point out a few things. Within the pages of this book, you will hear about difficult experiences and troubling situations. I encourage you to push through because there is definitely a proverbial light at the end of this tunnel. I also want to say that my thoughts and recollections are not meant to hurt anyone. These are my memories and reflections and if you were a part of any of them, you are welcome to disagree or have a different opinion. However, you are also welcome to laugh, cry, and reminisce with me and simply grasp hope with me. My purpose in sharing my story is to help even one other person out there realize they are not alone. They are not crazy. They, too, can weather the storms of this life and come out on the other side better for having not only survived but realizing that they, too, are a new creation. Without further ado... let's Carpe Spero!

"The strongest oak tree of the forest is not the one that is protected from the storm and hidden from the sun. It's the one that stands in the open where it is compelled to struggle for its existence against the winds and rains and the scorching sun."
Napoleon Hill[1]

Chapter One

There is this song by Savage Garden called, "Two Beds and a Coffee Machine".[2] It's about a mom and a couple of kids running from a horrific life. As I am making coffee in my hotel room in a strange place called Pocatello, Idaho, this song comes to mind; I realize I am her, and it is now my song. I look over as my sons are sleeping in the bed next to mine, and all I can think of is that I must have lost my mind. We barely know where we are headed, I have a few hundred dollars to my name, and the car is full of the basics for survival... this is crazy. I sip my coffee, lift a few prayers, and shed a few tears. The boys are awake now, and it's time to move on.

Windows down. Music playing while the air freshens the messy car. Along the road there are several types of trees. Pines, evergreens, maples... and they get my memories going into overdrive. When I was young, I believe it was at the end of sixth grade camp, we were given redwood saplings to take home. Now, Redwoods or Sequoias are not supposed to be able to grow down in Southern California and definitely not with a little girl who has been known to kill a cactus. However, my sapling sprouted roots and grew out of its original home, a Styrofoam cup, into a planter and then into the center of our backyard. We took family pictures with this Sequoia, and it grew to be a beautiful centerpiece within my family's outdoor space. Even after I left, my Sequoia kept growing. I was living overseas when I got a call from my dad explaining that my Sequoia would have to be taken out. I cried; this little sapling and I had grown up and experienced so many things together - how could it be chopped down? Alas, Sequoias are a protected species of tree and therefore the city would pay for it to, instead, be uprooted and replanted back in the National Redwood Forest. My Sequoia is still growing to this day. Like me, it was moved from its original environment yet found a way to thrive and grow even when its soil was hostile. We make a Symbian Circle, this unlikely pair - a girl and her tree.

As I come back to reality, I am somehow emboldened by this flashback with my Sequoia. Except, now I am not alone. There are two other saplings in the picture, and we have been uprooted and are running for our very lives to a place completely foreign to us. This memory has once again given me hope that even though we don't know what tomorrow holds, we are together. We will find a way to get rooted and grow despite hostilities, fears, tears and unknown circumstances. We will grow together - stronger and healthier - just like my Sequoia. This new forest we are headed towards will be what we make of it. Tonight, we will find rest in two more beds with another coffee machine.

With my sapling Sequoia for high school graduation

---

[1] Hill, N. (n.d.). *The strongest oak tree of the forest is not the one that is protected from the storm and hidden from the sun…*

[2] Hayes, D., & Jones, D. (1999). *Two beds and a coffee machine* [Song]. On *Affirmation*. Columbia Records.

"Finding joy in the shade of Sequoias."
Unknown[3]

Chapter Two

Upon reaching the Pacific Northwest, we were like fish out of water. The boys had only known about small town life, and when I say small, I mean tiny. The population sign for our previous hometown claimed 1,500, but we all knew that was only because they counted the cows and the hunters. So, this beautiful valley we found ourselves in boasted about 50,000 back in the mid-2000s, and the neighboring city was more like 300,000. As far as my sons were concerned, they had moved to Gotham City, and Batman was nowhere to be found.

Despite the fact that things could have been much worse, we were still alone. Part of why we chose this destination was that we knew no one here, so no one would think to look for us here. A previous family member had bought a home near a lake that they were hoping to eventually retire to, but it was subsequently not being lived in. It was our perfect shelter. No bills in our names, no bank accounts, no way to trace us.

We covered our tracks. We had school records sent to four different locations before eventually reaching us. The boys' schools were all on high alert for strangers or anyone asking too many questions, and we had escape routes in place. The local YWCA gave us all cell phones so we could reach each other in a moment's notice. I got the boys into counseling right away, then began to think about how I was going to start work.

Shortly after settling in, the first storm hit. I had taken a trip back to our former home so I could file taxes and gather some belongings I had stored in a neighboring town. As I was coming back, I had a freak accident and fell on my right hand. It was crumpled up under my body, and when I looked at it, bones were sticking out. Severe nerve damage and three surgeries later, I found myself wondering how I was ever going to provide for myself, let alone my children.

One day, I stood in front of the mailbox and saw an advertisement for a program called Changepoint[4]. It was offered at the local community college for women in transition. I began laughing and crying, rushed home and signed up. I had been in the hospitality industry for most of my life, this required two working hands and a much more physically healthy body than I currently had, but Changepoint was just what I needed. I was a broken woman, not only physically but mentally and especially, spiritually. Our instructors were amazing and patient. I met other broken and afraid women, and in this spectacular program we grew together. Women in the Changepoint Program were educated in self-confidence, basic computer skills, self-defense, interview skills, resume writing, budgeting and so much more. Just like my Sequoia, we were all being replanted, given water and sunlight and - wow - despite the hostile environments we had all just run from, we were seizing new opportunities and moving forward into new, healthy arenas.

The women's group leader encouraged me to go back to

school full-time! I had taken an aptitude test, and it mentioned being a movie director...hahaha. It also suggested I try my hand at politics. I literally laughed out loud. A single mom in hiding, throwing herself out to the public eye. Nope, not gonna happen. The third thing the test said I would be good at was teaching. Why not? I went for it, wrote for every grant and scholarship available and applied to every college in the state.

I am reminded at this juncture of a conversation with a friend. Choosing a college was no easy task. Who knew I would be accepted to every university? I narrowed it down to a local university which, I felt, aligned with my spiritual background. It was small, inviting and was offering an Excellence Scholarship. However, my friend challenged me to consider a private university whose spiritual alignment was different from mine but was considered a leader in education while also having a more prestigious community. I honestly didn't think about them because I thought they were out of my league. I plucked up courage and applied. I remember getting my acceptance letter and jumping for joy with my sons in the kitchen. My boys were so excited for me. I chose this university and proceeded to strive for a BA in History and Theater. There are so many good things to mention about this time as a non-traditional student and more symbiotic moments between myself and my Sequoia.

There is this process where a tree binds itself to an object and, as time passes, the tree simply flows around the object. I feel as if I did this with education. Time and life were passing by, but my opportunities in higher education simply blossomed and engulfed my current life. Not in an obsessive way but in the most unlikely, yet healthy branch. Going back to school later in life has its ups and downs.

As a single parent, I went to class when my sons were in school, then didn't crack a book until they hit the sack. I wrote my papers late into the night and fumbled my way through technological advances with programs and apps I had never used; Dropbox, Twitter and Facebook were truly becoming platforms I was expected to know and use. I felt, for the first time in my personal life, I had to adapt or die. This meant, for me, figuring out a detailed schedule. Setting myself and my sons up the night before for success. Clothes were picked out, shoes by the door, backpacks thoroughly gone through, then after finishing up my own homework, rest. The alarm would go off about 6:30 AM, and the morning routine of a Drill Sergeant ensued. My boys could sleep through World War III and it took an act of God to get them moving, teeth brushed, breakfast and out the door. Once everyone was deposited at their appropriate schools, I had one last chance to look over my homework and print all my research/essays, grab coffee and engage with my professors and friends. I rarely went home between classes, because, if I did, life would drag my attention away from my studies. So, when the boys were in school, I could be found somewhere on campus studying like a mad woman. Pick up the boys, their friends, snacks, homework and video games - if it wasn't wrestling season. Then, feeding three to six boys, it was like feeding a small third world country. Take friends home, shower and maybe catch a show before crashing and getting ready to do it all again the next day. Raquel Welch is quoted as saying, "I was not a classic mother. But my kids were never palmed off to boarding school. So, I didn't bake cookies. You can buy cookies, but you can't buy love."[5]

Later in my journey, I would teach a class for Single Parents. I mentioned to all my students that it's important to pick one thing each month that's helpful to yourself. At that time in my journey, I chose housekeeping. There was a woman in church looking for work and since I needed the help, I hired her to come twice a month to clean. This gave me a clean home and more time to focus on my boys. At different times, forms of self-care adapted, from massages and manicures, to home spa nights, depending on budget and current needs. Because I was an older student, my professors became my best friends and mentors. They enriched my life in a way I could never have imagined. Life became full, and honestly, the intensity and speed at which I approached life was Mach 2. As unhealthy as it was, the boys and I were surviving, so I kept pushing. I kept up the break-neck pace and ignored my body, mind, and soul, which was shattered beyond recognition by this point in my journey.

Often in my reading, I come across a book which impacts me deeply. Recently I read one called *Scared Sick.*[6] The authors, Meredith Wiley and Robin Karr-Moss, speak of how even though on the outside a child who comes from trauma appears to be competent, successful, outgoing and confident, there is actually an undercurrent of anxiety and perfectionism which runs deep. This deeply resonated with me. The authors also shared that when concern comes to the traumatized, it is automatically seen as a sign of weakness. Each passing decade adds depression, fear, lack of confidence and a deep-seeded feeling of being unworthy. These emotions affect their view and expectations of others as well as traumatically affecting their physical health. Trust and secure attachments are beyond difficult, and thus, they find a need to create false security blankets. I will reveal more of how this affected me personally in more depth throughout upcoming chapters. Suffice it to say, unbeknownst to me, these emotions, physical afflictions and false securities were about to collide and stop me dead in my tracks.

I feel this may be an appropriate time to recognize some fantastic women who came into my life at this point in my journey. These women are still in my life today, and I cannot imagine not having them with me in this journey we call life. Stacy, my history professor, floated into class. Honestly, I judged this book by her cover. Her hair was in fantastic dreads; her clothes were all mismatched and flowing; outside of films and shows, I don't think I had ever met a person who personified what I imagined a hippie to look like. I knew right away I was going to have to switch classes, because I was unsure, we could never be on the same page - especially within history or politics. However, by the end of the first class, I was challenged both intellectually and culturally, and decided maybe - just maybe - I could learn something from this hippie. One of my favorite but most challenging things we did in her class was called a junkie. We, basically, had to take our readings and place them in a historical fiction viewpoint. It demonstrated that you had done the reading, but, even more importantly, you could understand and give the history life. I also learned how to do my first annotated bibliography, which was so difficult at first but something else I came to love and respect. As the semester wore on, I became increasingly impressed with this hippie, and, by the end of the term, I sought her out in friendship. Coffees, lunches, trips and the most amazing relationship ever came from simply opening my heart and mind to new possibilities.

My dearest friends continued to come to me in unexpected packages. Tina and I could not be more opposite. Where I was chatty, nervous and serious, Tina was introverted, humble, completely unassuming, funny and deeply complex. Those are just a few examples of the inner workings of one of the most amazing women I have been blessed to call my friend. We met in the theater, which I ended up in by chance (more on that later). Tina and her crazy husband attended school together, and, in the theater, you grew to be an extended family. Hours and hours of rehearsal, learning lines, costumes, makeup (alongside laughter and tears) frustration and exultation forged our bonds. If you know, you know. Every emotion at one point or another is tapped into.

Tina had three girls, and I had two boys. Since Tina and I were always busy together, our children were together all the time and naturally gravitated toward each other. One day my son came to me and told me he was going to ask Coral (Tina's middle daughter) to be his girlfriend. I panicked because I didn't want to lose my friend if these two kids decided they were moving on from one another. Tina and I discussed it and were determined that no matter what, we would remain friends. It was not easy to do as we are both protective momma bears, but we were resolute in our desire to remain friends. Our youngest two decided to try their hand at the dating game, and we all survived that inevitable breakup. Thank Goodness our kids are all grown up now and still remain friends to this day.

Tina was studying at Eastern Washington University to be a counselor, and I was attending Gonzaga for a degree in teaching. The distance didn't seem to matter; we remained close throughout our years of studying, and she is my greatest confidant to this day. So much so, that years later when I needed a professional counselor for my podcast, I sought her out because I knew she would be a perfect fit. Whenever I need sound advice, a listening ear and some frank but unconditional love, I find it in Tina.

Speech 101 was a required course on my degree path. As I was reluctantly sitting in this new class, asking myself "how in the world was this class going to help me in real life?" I met another lifelong friend and mentor. Ron, or Professor Heiss, was so much fun. Most days, I left class laughing and pondering some new quotes or challenging concepts. We had to find poems that are related to our lives, give demonstration speeches, then something a bit more challenging; something a bit more personal. I chose to talk about the girl next door who was going through unimaginable things. A lot of people would walk away from her or not want to listen to her situation, but some would listen with compassion. I encouraged my classmates to engage rather than turn away and told them they never knew who this girl next door might be. It could even be the one standing in front of them. Once again, throughout the semester, I grew close to one of my professors. At the end of the semester, Ron asked if I had ever been a stage manager. I didn't even know what that was, but Ron assured me I would be good at it and asked if I would be interested in joining the theater crew. Wow! Theater was never something that had crossed my mind, which is kind of strange having grown up a California girl surrounded by celebrities. My mother grew up three doors down from John Wayne in Belmont Shores, and I grew up watching John Stamos in a garage band with the Bardwell Brothers. I knew John before he was Blackie or Uncle Jessie. I loved Broadway plays, music of any kind, dancing and movies but had never thought of working within the industry so to speak. I loved being a stage manager because it was all about order and helping my cast and crew be successful. Later, I was blessed to be assistant director, then even tried my hand at acting. Casting shows was the most fun, deciding who would make the best actor or actress for each role is complicated and engaging. My sons were able to join me on set, making our connections stronger. Who would have thought? I enjoyed it so much that when I arrived at Gonzaga, I chose to continue to pursue theater as part of my degree. Something I have never regretted. Thanks, Ron.

With my boys, when they were young

[3] Finding joy in the shade of sequoias. (n.d.).

[4] Changepoint Northwest Center for Housing. (n.d.). Changepoint Northwest Center for Housing (Washington nonprofit corporation; UBI No. 604122231). Administratively dissolved in 2021.

[5] Welch, R. (n.d.). *I was not a classic mother. But my kids were never palmed off to boarding school. So, I didn't bake cookies. You can buy cookies, but you can't buy love.* FixQuotes. https://fixquotes.com/quotes/i-was-not-a-classic-mother-but-my-kids-were-never-64258/

[6] Karr-Morse, R., & Wiley, M. S. (2012). *Scared sick: The role of childhood trauma in adult disease*. Basic Books.

"In every walk with nature, one receives more than they seek."
John Muir[7]

Chapter Three

One fine fall day, my world came to a screeching halt. It was not that I didn't comprehend what it meant to suffer illness or injury. Two C-sections, a hysterectomy and an oophorectomy, I knew what it meant to have health issues which could affect you long after they were over and done with. Just to get through school and my new life in Washington, it took three orthopedic surgeries and to this day I still suffer the effects of massive nerve damage. In fact, when I finally went to apply for disability a few years later, it was actually all the damage done to my hands that helped my case; more on that later.

I had recently undergone surgery for the removal of my gallbladder. I actually thought I was on the road to recovery. Previously, surgeries had been complex and full of issues. There is this great book I recently read called *The Body Keeps the Score.*[8] It made sense of my body's complicated responses to illness and surgeries. I had no idea just how much it would explain the revelations I was about to encounter with my surgeon. I had my two-week follow-up jammed into my busy afternoon of theater, kids and papers. In my mind, the surgeon was lucky I could squeeze him in. Besides, I felt great! Not a care in the world. Dramatic Pause. The surgeon wants to go back to his office. No thanks, but I slowly follow as my heart rate is starting to accelerate. The surgeon explains that while he was inside removing my gallbladder, he caught a glimpse of my liver, and he didn't like what he saw. I was sure at that moment I turned green. Could he see me panicking? He had taken a biopsy and just received the results. Drumroll, the biopsy confirmed cirrhosis with some stage four cells already present. Wait a minute, isn't cirrhosis for drunks and ex-druggies? Nope.

Actually, there are 47 different kinds of liver disease; I seemed to have two underlying causes for mine. Cirrhosis of the liver, for those who don't know, is simply late-stage scarring or fibrosis. My doctor wanted to set me up with the closest thing we had in this town to a liver specialist, and they would take it from there. To top it off, he said the scans confirmed there were cancerous cells beginning to form. Great doc - let's save the best for last, ugh! Then he asked if I had any questions? Yes, but my mind couldn't seem to form them into any semblance of cohesion at this moment.

I walked out the door, promised to make an appointment with the specialist and drove my way back to campus. We were in the middle of a play; I believe it might have been *Fahrenheit 451*. I needed to eat but couldn't seem to find the motivation. Instead, I curled up by a window in the foyer of the theater staring mindlessly out the window as it began to rain. Emily, a fellow theater student, couldn't help but notice me (I must have looked pretty lost) and stopped to ask if I had eaten already. No. She asked if I wanted to grab something with her as we had a full night ahead of dress rehearsal and chaos. The boys would be walking up to campus later to eat dinner, attempt homework and hang out with my theater friends. Sure, I should eat something. I know Emily was talking, but I honestly don't know if I heard what she was saying. There was a pause, and I blurted out that I had just been diagnosed with cancer and cirrhosis. She stopped, hugged me and asked how she could help. Thanks for the offer, but I am sure it will be fine; thanks for the concern. Let's eat!

I surreptitiously moved the conversation away from anything too serious. I was ready to move on. Not really, but I did not know what else to do. What I really wanted to do was run to the highest point on campus and scream out to the world to Stop! How was I supposed to blindly move forward when my health seemed to be screaming at me to stop dead in my tracks? What was I supposed to tell my sons? Sorry boys, but after all the hell we have already lived through, I may not be around to even see you graduate from school - never mind weddings, grandbabies and all the other things most parents have to look forward to. I was scared, but rather than give in to what I considered to be weakness and self-pity, I simply found another mask to put on for the rest of the world. I read a poem many years ago, when I was young; it had to do with the masks we choose to wear for safety, for fear, for protection, for survival and even those as simple as assisting us in social situations. We all wear masks, but mine had become stifling and completely unhealthy. It was lovely, and the smile was sincere - at least on the outside. On the inside, however, it was suffocating. If you want to know more about the masks that we wear, I encourage you to check out my podcast called Behind the Mask[9] wherein myself and a couple of friends really dig into why we wear masks, good, bad and otherwise.

I ran into Emily the next day between classes, and she was insistent that what I really needed was a Bible Study. Seriously, girl? I could lead a Bible study. Besides, I did not have time for more promises that were clearly not meant for me. God and I had been battling in my heart for quite some time now. I had concluded that, despite His words, I was obviously created to be abused, neglected and taken advantage of. In fact, I think by this point in life, I was wearing a neon sign on my forehead letting the world know I was here to be mistreated - free of charge, cost paid by the victim - me. Emily was still blathering on about the wonderful women she would invite to this Bible study and asked when I was free to go. I think, simply to get her to shut-up, I said "how about next week?" I even agreed to meet at my least favorite coffee shop, which begins with an 'S' and shall remain unnamed. I'm not sure why, but I showed up despite my desire to cancel.

Emily's mother, Verlinda, a lovely woman named Chris and Emily were present. Although warm and inviting, I had on my proper mask of the socialite. Then, against my better judgment, I agreed to a second study. Furthermore, I agreed that if I could drag my sons out of bed, I would show up Sunday morning for church. By showing up Sunday, I could kill two birds with one stone. One of my religious classes was requiring me to attend a liturgical service from a denomination I had never been to. This would definitely qualify, then I could write the stupid response, get my A and mollify my new friends.

Service was at 10 AM. I miraculously got the boys dressed and out the door. Emily and the other women were so excited I had showed up. I almost felt guilty for my plans to break their hearts, because this was not something I wished to engage in for any length of time. Boy, I was wrong. The worship was amazing, and I think at one point I almost cried. I had missed good worship, and these folks seemed to have such sincere hearts as they sang. The pastor steps up to the podium, and in concert, everyone pulls out notebooks and Bibles like a class full of students. It felt inspiring, and was a totally new spiritual experience.

By the way, I did get an A on my paper. It was probably my

third study in; Emily was reading some scriptures aloud and wanted me to understand that we were all born into light. NO! There was no light for my entry into this nightmarishly dark world, and no scripture was going to change my mind. I didn't believe these women could truly grasp my dark thoughts and feelings, so I chose to remain silent. I was giving my typical Sunday school answers in most of the studies. I had grown up surrounded by religion, but it never resembled the relationship these women were presenting to me. I continued to keep my spiritual mask in place, and Emily was the only one who seemed to see past it. She even challenged me a couple times to stop giving her my simple responses and to tell her what I truly was thinking and feeling. I upped my mask game and gave her a little deeper thoughts but was not honestly ready to dig deep. That was way too scary for these women but even more so for me. I gave these women just enough. It wasn't that I didn't want a relationship with God, but trust and hope were very difficult concepts for my broken heart to grasp, even with all the love these women were sharing. I was baptized about nine months later and jumped into my servant role right out of the gate.

Some of you may wonder, why would I choose to get baptized again after all this time and although I had grown up in the church. I viewed this baptism as a very personal choice to begin a relationship with my Lord and Savior. Not something my father, family or friends had chosen for me but something *I* wanted. It was years later, but a sister in the faith also pointed out to me that my first baptism was filled with trauma. As I came out of the water the first time, I was staring into the face of one of my biggest abusers. It definitely, whether or not I knew it at the time, affected my early walk with God. Although I desired this relationship, my fears, my past, my trauma responses still won the day but only for a time. I promise, more on this later.

Once again, not digging too deep, just enough not to be noticed and fly under the proverbial radar. No one asked too many questions, and the boys and I had gotten good at surface relationships. My boys were obviously skeptical but trusted me. They each have their own spiritual journeys, and I encourage you to ask them if you are ever given the opportunity. Suffice it to say, from this point forward, Jesus was very much a part of my life and thus the boys'. And there are no regrets. I found one of my prayers from this time and thought it might just explain where I was in my new walk with God.

> *Control. I am afraid of losing it. The thought makes me feel vulnerable and weak. Father, please help me. I don't know how to let go and trust You. I am afraid that You might ask me to surrender all. I know and believe that You are good and kind but I tremble when I can't see the next step or if the path ahead is dark. Help me to trust You. Teach me to trust You for I have never learned. I feel sometimes as if I have been running all my life and I am so tired. I want to stop. I want to throw myself into Your arms and let everything go. Please help me, Father, because I am afraid of what might happen if I abandon my control. Please show Yourself to me. I want to see You. Thank You for the reminder in 1 John 4:18 that where Your love is, there is no fear because Your perfect love casts out all fear. Amen*

Here will be another great opportunity to share impactful relationships. I would like to return to two women already mentioned in my journey. Verlinda was Emily's mother and became one of my greatest friends and mentors. Verlinda was also a single mother, a woman who had survived too many things to recount here, but, more importantly, a woman who desired to love and help others. Then, there is Chris, another single mom, but, like me, of two sons. These women loved me and met me where I was at. I don't know about you, but I love to keep special cards and letters. I recently came across one from Chris, who is unfortunately no longer with us. She lost her battle with cancer over a decade ago, and there is not a day that goes by that I don't miss her beautiful smile and her sweet words of encouragement.

She wrote, "I am so full of awe, I finally can truly call you sister. Sharing your love of life and your joy in the Lord has been an exciting adventure and I am looking forward to the next part of our journey." Chris was a sister of my heart and one of my closest friends. To know I brought her joy as she did me was just the reminder I needed to keep putting one foot in front of the other. So, finding this particular card was truly a little slice of heaven.

Over coffee, I think if we had put our three minds to it, we could have solved world hunger and peace. All joking aside, we did work together to help ourselves and others through things like Mission Kitchen[10], HOPEworldwide[11], and A Single Mom's Ministry all while holding down jobs, continuing our education, raising kids, laughing so hard our sides hurt, crying tears through Chemo Slumber Parties and losing friends and loved ones. Chris and Verlinda would often be with me as I was in and out of the hospital. We would crack jokes, throw peanuts and keep the hospital staff on their toes. I would not be standing here today without these friendships. These relationships with my fellow giant Sequoias were what helped me not only survive but thrive.

Fall on campus at my alma mater

[7] Muir, J. (1918). *Steep trails*. Houghton Mifflin. [vault.sierraclub.org]

[8] van der Kolk, B. A. (2014). *The body keeps the score: Brain, mind, and body in the healing of trauma. Viking.

[9] Frederiksen, E. E., Leigh, L., & van Zandt, T. (n.d.). *Behind the Mask PC* [Audio podcast].Spotify. https://open.spotify.com/show/1OZ2Dba6qOkEETBVRS0En

[10] Mission Kitchen. (n.d.). *Mission Kitchen*. Spokane, WA. [datanyze.com]

[11] HOPE worldwide. (n.d.). *HOPE worldwide.* https://www.hopeww.org/ [hopeww.org]

"Storms make trees take deeper roots."
Dolly Parton[12]

Chapter Four

Back to my health battle. Within the first year, I had been set up with a specialist who removed my cancerous cells but didn't really have many answers to my questions, except that I probably had about two to five years before my liver took its last gasp. I began having blood drawn every 90 days to monitor my liver and other health issues. There were all kinds of new medications prescribed, and my body often did not respond well. Nausea, vomiting, dizziness, more migraines - not to mention that I did not have the best medical insurance throughout this process. When you are a poor single mom, it's Medicaid, and your choices and options are extremely limited. This time of our life was fraught with anxiety and more unknowns than knowns.

As I have mentioned before, there were multiple hospital visits, a new diagnosis of diabetes and the migraines were so numerous at this point that it became debilitating. Remember my mention of the book, *The Body Keeps the Score*? Well, my body was in overdrive, and the score was: body 99 to Lori's health 1. With the help and suggestion of one of my professors at Gonzaga, friends and family raised money, and I was able to get a second opinion down in Phoenix, AZ at the Mayo Clinic. Gonzaga wrote articles to raise awareness, and my church, professors and close friends opened a donation account for me through US Bank. I even wrote about it in my blog titled 'Carpe Spero' at one point, where I chronicled much of this part of my journey. The Mayo Clinic confirmed my diagnosis but also threw another log on the fire. I was significantly overweight, and until I could lose weight and get my diabetes under control, even if my liver disease progressed, I would be unable to get a transplant. Upon returning from the trip, I decided it would be best to get my affairs in order, get my will done and begin preparing for my inevitable death. I spoke with the boys, and as gently as possible, prepared them for the worst. We chose, as a family, to make the best of each moment and not focus on the dark possibilities.

So now you may be asking, what comes next? I sure did, and I really didn't have any answers. I was dying, and there did not seem to be much I or anyone else could do about it. As I have continuously alluded throughout this story already, I came from a long line of abuse. However, I have not spoken about how this manifested itself within my physical life. Somewhere along this journey, I had concluded that if I were larger, heavier, ugly on the outside then men would leave me alone and women would no longer be jealous. Growing up, I had a fantastic body. I wasn't the tiny, petite Barbie. No, I was more like Marilyn Monroe, Skipper. I had the boobs, hips and athletic legs of a runner/surfer girl. I was also blessed with an extroverted, social skill which too often got misconstrued as flirting. I simply loved people, but most of the women in my life were jealous, and the men wouldn't keep their hands off.

Unfortunately, the world and its unrealistic expectations for women played right into this. Men were actually no longer bothering me, and the women in my life were no longer threatened by my naturally flirtatious nature and previously beautiful body. My relationship with food became truly unhealthy and completely driven by fear, emotions and my totally unrealistic need for perfection. I ate to prove I was unworthy, then I would throw up in shame. I ate to feed unmet feelings and emotions or scare off irrational fears, then I would beat myself up mentally for having given in so easily. I ate out of loneliness, I ate out of boredom, I ate and I ate until I couldn't eat anymore. If I brought a package of cookies into the house, after the boys and their friends had some, I would quietly finish off the bag. It was like that with any leftovers. The boys and their friends would eat their fill, then in one sitting, I would finish whatever it was no matter how large a portion was left. It could be enough for one to three people. I didn't care. I just consumed it. All this was done in secret, never in front of anyone, including my sons. I was too ashamed but could not seem to stop myself. I was like an alcoholic with liquor, if there was excess food around, I would consume it, then more often than not, throw it up. I got to the stage in my disease where I no longer cared what I looked like or felt, then I just consumed it and felt ashamed of being such a glutton. It was a horrible, vicious cycle.

My diabetes was out of control, and, in my mind, just one more bit of proof that I was unworthy. I remember being so scared when I first pricked myself with the needle full of insulin, then years later when I did it repeatedly praying for an overdose so this awful life could simply just end. Migraines, low blood pressure, diabetes, complete lack of sleep, fuzzy brain and the list kept growing along with my weight. I was now over 350 pounds and dying, literally and figuratively. On the outside, I was so accomplished at wearing the happy, socialite mask that no one guessed the absolute chaos that was my true self. I hated myself and simply wished for God to just end this torture. Food and my insulin were going to help me end it all since God didn't seem to be listening. I had a few hospitalizations throughout this time, but no one seemed to catch on. So, I simply kept slowly killing myself.

On the outside, I was toxically happy and had gotten so good at wearing masks, speaking all the right words. Honestly, I am not sure what the right words were, but I knew I no longer knew or cared what they were; so long as no one knew what was actually going on in my mind and my heart. It sounds so ugly, but it was where I was in this part of my journey. As long as my family and friends were not able to discern my ugliness then I could just exist until God had mercy enough to let me end it all. I was rotting from the inside out.

By this time in my journey, I was really good at wearing a mask. I didn't truly let people in because I did not trust them. That would have been too dangerous in my mind. Up to this point, lack of trust was a survival mechanism, but it had finally stopped being about survival. It was more about how long I could exist in this way. It was not until I became a student later in life that I realized I wasn't alone in all these ugly thoughts.

While I was doing research for a speech 101 assignment, I discovered that 14 to 15 percent of women[13] will visit an emergency room related to some form of domestic violence.[14] Every nine seconds[15] nearly a third of homeless women and children in this country are fleeing from domestic violence.[16] One of the scariest facts of all is that 30% of women who are murdered in the U.S. are murdered by their husbands, ex-husbands or boyfriends. Incest and Childhood trauma is clearly associated with a higher risk of developing an eating disorder. Emotional Dysregulation, Lack of Coping Skills, Lack of Positive Body Image, Loss of Control and Safety and - interestingly - a connection of poor bonds with their mothers was found in a significant number of survivors of incest.

All of this information was found online, and unfortunately, is an even more significant and prevalent problem today. I mention all this to say, those of us who have survived are clearly not alone. There is a reason we ended up where we are at, but I also say all that to remind myself that I choose not to be a victim anymore.

These musings bring to mind one of my favorite scriptures. "Now faith is the substance of things hoped for, the evidence of things not seen." Hebrews 11:1 (NKJV) I believe hope, faith, joy, love and sorrow are not for the faint of heart. There is nothing casual about creation or death. Many years ago, I chose to leave the classroom of casual inquiry and enrolled in the one for diligent seekers. What this meant in my life was that sometimes, more than I care to count, answers have been withheld from me.

The older and wiser I get, the less I believe this is for my harm or harassment and rather more for my benefit and reward. I cling to a hope that is eternal. As I approach each new day, I can rejoice that my cup runs over with a complete and whole life only gained through my willingness to fly a little blind most days. Thus, I am, at the very least promised, an eventful life full of hope for the very best. I choose a new life, transformation and to Carpe Spero; Seize Hope. I didn't come to this space easily but with true conviction and a desire to change my outcome. That is what is at the heart of my story. Let's continue...

In 2018, my body finally gave up the battle. I had a stroke, which they never were able to diagnose exactly where it came from. It was a full body neurological event which affected my speech and my ability to walk and move my limbs from the neck down - honestly the scariest health event ever! Can you imagine not desiring anyone touching your body, and now you can't eat, go to the bathroom or shower without assistance? Now, my sons, caregivers and any semblance of independence truly came screeching to a halt.

I actually re-wrote my will and asked for a DNR (do not resuscitate) and to say I re-wrote it is to say one of my best friends had to do that for me as I couldn't type it. Talk about being an unconditionally, loving friend. These are the types of folks you need by your side, and God has given them to me in abundance. Emily and my boys had to process what it was like to witness your mother/best friend going from an active participant in her life to one who needed constant care. The boys each had to deal with their own trauma of witnessing the stroke and subsequent ride to the hospital, then doctors who were less than helpful. Thank goodness for Emily, Verlinda, Kevin and others being my advocates in my time of distress. Because I wasn't presenting as a traditional stroke victim, we had medical staff that didn't believe it to be a stroke, so they tried to treat me as a drug addict or other mentally unstable patient.

My advocates fought for me until we got the right hospital and team of specialists realized this was a major neurological event and I needed help. There is so much I don't remember from that time. I do remember everyone agreeing I was surely dying, but amazingly enough it wasn't my liver. Despite my low self-esteem, God and my loved ones made sure I knew how much I was actually loved. Once again, even though life circumstances were dark, my fellow Sequoias were resolute in their love for me. Thus God kept asking me to put down deeper roots and stand firm.

Another amazing part of this journey was the relationships I built with the nurses, therapists and doctors who respected me, showed love and care to myself, my family and friends. I wouldn't have gotten through this event without their top-notch level of care. We exchanged stories, laughter, journals, cards and so much joy and triumph together.

Roots of resiliency

---

[12] Parton, D. (n.d.). *Storms make trees take deeper roots.* [southernliving.com]

[13] Thomas, B. (2017, October 16). *Emergency departments often are first point of care for domestic violence trauma, injury cases.* **ACEP Now**.
https://www.acepnow.com/article/emergency-departments-often-first-point-care-domestic-violence-trauma-injury-cases/

[14] National Coalition Against Domestic Violence. (2015). *Domestic violence national statistics.* https://www.ncadv.org/ [wck.org]

[15] National Network to End Domestic Violence. (n.d.). *Domestic violence, housing, and homelessness.*
https://blog.homelessinfo.org/wp-content/uploads/NNEDV-Fact-Sheet.pdf

[16] Smith, E. L. (2022). *Female murder victims and victim–offender relationship, 2021* (NCJ 305613). Bureau of Justice Statistics, U.S. Department of Justice.
https://bjs.ojp.gov/female-murder-victims-and-victim-offender-relationship-2021

"The Sequoia is a powerful and courageous spirit that balances destruction and creation."
Laurel Wauters[17]

Chapter Five

It would not be out of line to question exactly how I had found myself in this current state. When I wasn't too afraid, I asked myself, but the answers were always so dark and dysfunctional that I never knew what to do with them. I had had a few counselors over the years, but even with them, I would only let them in so far. I had gotten so good at giving the answers professionals wanted to hear. My abuse and neglect had started out of the womb, so it's difficult to know where to begin. Much of what I have been told about my life up to the age of five is simply sad. A biological mother who could not be bothered with motherhood. She seemed to love her alcohol and long-haul truck driver who was, himself, addicted to drugs and rarely present. I had a biological uncle who molested me and several other children.

By the time my little sister was born, I had been left at truck stops, with grandparents, other family members and complete strangers. There was no real home base and no loving family. By the age of three, I was changing diapers and feeding a newborn while abuse and neglect continued.

My biological mother eventually realized she didn't want children and gave me (four years old) and my sister (one year old) up for adoption. About a year later, there was this lovely woman who desired a beautiful baby girl and my little sister was her heart's desire. She wanted to do her Christian duty and would also take in the older sister (me), but I learned right away that I had to earn my place, even in this new environment. I was simply lucky to be given this opportunity. No more truck stops and strange homes. There were so many toys, a huge, beautiful home and three older brothers.

My adoptive mother could never imagine exactly what she was getting herself into. That adorable baby girl and her older sister had night terrors, didn't have much grasp on even basic language and, apparently, I was so uncouth. No manners and I could curse a barmaid under the table. When my sister had nightmares, she came to me. I held her, comforted her and would still change a diaper all to my new mother's chagrin and complete frustration. She and I constantly seemed to be at odds as to who exactly the parent was. I eventually gave in out of sheer preservation, because my new mother seemed to have no control of her emotions or temper. Whenever I didn't act exactly as I should, I was hit with whatever was handy: shoes, hangers, hands and the like. If that didn't do the trick, as I aged, I was grounded from anything which might be considered fun.

I remember when my mother finally realized that grounding me was actually a perfect opportunity for me to run away in my mind through books. She took away every pleasure book, which left history, religion, encyclopedias and dictionaries. I have read them all from cover to cover. Reading of any kind could take me out of all the insanity which was my life. Reading has always been my favorite form of escape.

The abuse wasn't only physical; my sweet Christian mother could also curse a barmaid under the table, but only for a private audience. She was a taskmaster of horrific proportions. Punishment was often handed down in the form of scrubbing grout with a toothbrush or pulling weeds. Don't misunderstand, everyone in my generation did chores; it was the way in which these chores were handed out. On my knees, in the hottest part of the day, having to perform the tasks multiple times because it would never be good enough. It was the disdain and anger behind each punishment, the fear of further punishment if the task was not completed in a timely manner to absolute perfection, and all while she was looming over my shoulder, pushing, prodding and belittling me throughout.

Being in the kitchen with her was absolute torture. Here, perfectionism once again ruined any childhood fun which many children get to experience. I couldn't figure out the measurements quickly enough, so I must obviously be an imbecile. If I spilled or dropped something, then I was too clumsy and practically useless. I remember a time when I tried to scramble some eggs, and they were too runny. My mother took the plate around to show everyone in the family my failure. I tried to bake some biscuits, but once again, my failure was used by the family - instigated by my mother - as an example of what not to do. My brothers used them for hockey pucks while I watched in utter shame and disgrace. As a result, from a young age, I avoided the kitchen at all costs. If I could fly under the radar and hang with the boys and watch or participate in sports, that's where I could be found. I kept stats at my brother's baseball games. After setting the perfect table, I was allowed to watch football on the holidays or the Olympics with my grandmothers. As I grew up, I joined every school activity possible: choir, drama, track and field, volleyball, tennis - anything to get me away from the house or my family.

Then, there were all the social expectations. With money comes unrealistic expectations of perfection: perfect clothes, perfect words, perfect grades, perfect weight, teeth, hair... "ladies don't sweat, they glisten". We would never dream of walking out the door without every hair in place and our faces on. "Ladies don't engage in unsavory conversations of personal nature," she would say. Emotions are always kept in check; we can laugh, but not too loudly. Our body is trained not to engage in any natural bodily function; sneezing is a delicate affair. If we have hiccups or gas, we figure out how to hold it in or leave the room until we can get it under control. Eating became a fine art, and I often heard, "a lady never ever indulges or turns up her nose. We must eat anything placed in front of us and find something praiseworthy in it. Our home, clothes and smiles reflect us, but more importantly, our family. Our family reputation is all that matters, and at all costs must be upheld."

I hated car rides to and from any family or social event. We were grilled on who we were allowed to speak with, who deserved our attention and who did not, exactly how much to drink and eat, how to sit and to be ready to leave at a moment's notice, because it was rude to keep people waiting. Afterwards, it was the tortuous ride home where we were berated for every way in which we failed to be perfect and make the family look good. It was exhausting and discouraging. There was no way to meet the unrealistic standards set before us, but I would die trying. I truly wanted to please my family, not only to not get punished, but on a deep psychological level. All I wanted was to be loved. So, I would keep trying to earn it, because at that age, I thought it was the only way to survive.

I feel the need to stop here and acknowledge that, as I have been writing this part of my life - laying it out there for all the world to see in the proverbial black and white - I find myself transported right back to all that trauma. Simply writing it all out has been its own trigger, if you will. I was nauseous, my hands were beginning to shake, my brain was aching as well as my heart, and I was almost overcome with tears. This is some tough stuff. I had to stop and take a few calming breaths and reset myself. I needed to acknowledge this is part of my legacy but not somewhere I needed to be stuck. The writing is filled with purpose and intention. No need for pity or tears.

Don't misunderstand, if I were reading or watching this story play out, I would probably shed some tears and want to comfort this young girl. In my mind, there is a difference between pity and empathy. As I noted earlier in my story, I know I am not alone in much of this tragedy, but I do not desire pity. I desire to have my words read and understood, if possible, and I feel pity often gets in the way of that. This part of my story needs to be told, recounted, then I can continue with my transformation.

Life is a balanced act. It has also been a great time for processing how I feel about adoption. I will not lie to you; there have been times throughout my life where I questioned why and how my adoption story unfolded. Upon reflection, though, the answers are still the same. Adoption is a part of my story for better or worse, and it is a part of how my life was woven into existence. I know this will sound cliche to some, but I honestly know that I would not be the woman before you without the trials, without the suffering, without the pain. We can't change the past, but we can embrace it, learn from it and use it as we boldly enter the next season of life. As a tree grows, it will have battles with wind and lack of water and nutrition, but as its roots are out there seeking, it will find the sun. It will find the water, and it will begin to grow again. And just like my Sequoia, I will survive.

A friend shared these words of wisdom with me, and I found them helpful and important enough to keep them as part of my story. Community trauma is as real as family trauma. Community care is part of healing. Let your audience care about you. That is not about pity. Pity means someone feels superior to the one suffering. Invite your audience to love you and those they see suffering around them. Those suffering are not less than. A Sequoia is not a lesser tree because it takes so long for it to grow and be fruitful. I am indeed not less or in need of pity, but I can recognize the power of community and realize my growth is often nurtured and excelled when surrounded by my fellow Sequoias. Thank you, SaraDawn.

I am also motivated by the power of poetry, and the powerful words written in Invictus come to my mind at this moment in time. "It matters not how straight the gate, how charged with punishments the scroll. I am the master of my fate: I am the captain of my soul."[18] If someone like Nelson Mandela can draw inspiration and resilience from such words, then so can we.[19]

Sitting in a tree

---

[17] Wauters, L. V. (n.d.). *Sequoia – courage.* **Tree Spirit Wisdom**. https://treespiritwisdom.com/tree-spirit-wisdom/sequoia-tree-symbolism/

[18] Henley, W. E. (1920). *Invictus.* In *Poems* (pp. 83–84). Macmillan. https://www.poetryfoundation.org/poems/51642/invictus

[19] Davis, A. (2025). What does the poem "Invictus" mean to Mandela? https://www.poemshubs.com/archives/13372

"He who plants a tree-plants hope."
Lucy Larcom[20]

Chapter Six

The next part of my story is no less harsh, but it must be shared to grasp the bitterness which almost permanently stopped my life. My adoptive mother's third husband, for all intents and purposes, is the closest thing I had to a father. He came into my life around the age of seven. He was everything I could have ever imagined a perfect daddy to be. He was generous, always had time for me and brought the whole family to church. He loved to teach me new things and taught me there was nothing I couldn't achieve if only I put my mind and heart into it. I used to visit him in the morning while he was reading the paper. He would read to me and even let me take sips of his coffee. In his lap, I felt so safe.

One day, his hand slipped under my nightgown. I didn't know what to do, so I froze. My father finished, pecked me on the forehead, and after, he assured me this was the way a daddy shows his princess his love for her. Then, he sent me back to my room.

He began coming into my room regularly. I never knew when and where he would appear. I felt as if I had no privacy, no safe place to retreat. The few times I had the temerity to ask him to stop; he would shift the focus to me and how I simply did not understand how much he loved me and how much he needed me. He developed close relationships with all my teachers, Sunday school teachers, school counselors, and administrators. These relationships were not for my benefit; they were to make sure I wasn't speaking to anyone, to show his dominance and control and to feed his obsessions. The molestations became a daily occurrence and more intense as the years went by. This, and so much more, went on from the age of eight up to age 16 when I finally got up the courage to say "STOP!" for the last time.

Upon further reflection, one of his common phrases came to mind while I was attempting to capture how my mind and heart were affected by this abusive man. To this day, when I am in a weakened state, I can still hear his words. "I am only doing what you want." As if I was somehow in control or desired to be abused/misused. I have been asked why I allowed this, how this made me feel and why it took me so long to put a stop to it? Let me respond with utter amazement. Did you ever feel like you could tell your father "no" at such a tender age? What kind of feelings were you feeling in your pre-teen years? My body had so many unknown feelings that, at times, I was overwhelmed. All I really wanted was to be loved, and this man assured me this was his way of showing me love. So, I accepted it, did not welcome it - and it was all my little body had ever known. Remember, my sexual abuse began long ago. By now, it was all I knew. Finally, let me ask you how long is too long or when is enough, enough?

For me, courage came in the form of my first boyfriend. Without knowing it, my future husband told me he loved me, and it didn't seem to come with any strings or weird physical attraction. We simply laughed, wrote love letters and went on double dates with friends. It was sweet and innocent and exactly what I needed to work up the courage to insist my father stop. However, when you stop an abuser, there is always a cost. I enjoyed protection from my mother, every piece of clothing I desired, trips, dinners and vacations. As long as I was pliable and performed well, as a princess, the world was my oyster. Now, my mother was back to free reign with her verbal abuse, and I could do nothing right. For both my parents, I could never live up to any standard, especially the absolute perfection which was expected. It did not stop me from trying. I so badly wanted to meet the mark.

Right before my senior year, things went really sideways. I was sitting at the table being lectured in some unknown way and I had missed the mark once again. My father's lecture was wrapping up, and his final words were, "And if you don't like it you can leave, young lady." As I walked back to my room, grounded for two weeks or more, something snapped in me. I went back to his final words. I could leave. Could I really? Where would I go? Who Cares? Anywhere had to be better than this. I quietly packed a bag and headed out the back door. I went around the corner to a girlfriend's house and asked if I could borrow the phone. This was the 80s and we did not all have cell phones yet. I called my boyfriend, who left work, and came immediately to my rescue. He took me to his parents where reality came crashing in. They couldn't let me stay there as they would be harboring a runaway. Although they believed my story, they didn't want to stand in the inevitable wrath of my father.

I found another family friend within the church who agreed to take me in but wanted me to chat with my youth pastor. I agreed, but he was friends with my father. So, I jumped the fence and ended up at my first teenage shelter. In tears, I shared my story and the police were called. Everyone but my family and church wanted to help me. Please forgive my church, as my father was an elder, a huge financial patron and leader within our Community. They were told I was simply a spoiled, dramatic child who surely could not be telling the truth. Besides, I was now a runaway, a student in trouble at school and had plans to marry my boyfriend as soon as possible. I personified trouble.

My mother and brothers finally heard me out. My middle brother was in the midst of his own young adult issues, and after suffering abuse of his own was saddened for me, but basically told me to move on, like he was doing. My eldest brother truly tried to help. He tried to convince my mother to leave her husband, but once he realized that was never going to happen, he also told me I simply needed to accept facts. He had his own issues and was a bit of a black sheep himself. He welcomed me to the club and wished me the best of luck. My little sister hated me, because now our family was under a microscope and she and mom were getting unwanted attention. I am sure from her point of view there were other reasons, but we never discussed them. From this point forward, our relationship was forever altered, and, in my opinion, has never fully recovered. I should make note here that when my sister and I were first adopted, we were inseparable.

Over the years, because of the dichotomous differences in how we were treated, my sister and I grew apart. She never received abuse from my mother, because she was my mother's greatest desire. I also believe she and my mother drew closer when the abuse and obsession with my father began. I honestly don't know, to this day, how much either of them witnessed or knew because we lived and survived in secrecy. It's difficult to imagine that they knew nothing.

Now, let's talk about my mother. My poor, broken mother. As I have shared, we had a difficult relationship before all this drama was added to the mix. At one point during my incestuous years, she had walked in, but my father and I assured her it wasn't what it looked like. Maybe she needed to believe that; I honestly do not know. By my teenage years, I felt in competition with my mother for attention, whether it was at church, school or with my father. When my father finally stopped protecting me, she zealously began making my life a living hell. At least this was my perspective. One of my close friends and I were watching a movie in a humanities class, and she remarked that it was crazy how they had made a movie about my mother. We laughed, but, in our minds, it was all too real.

The movie she was referring to was called *Mommy Dearest.* If you have never seen it, suffice it to say, this beautiful socialite adopts a little girl, then proceeds to torture and blame her for all that befalls her. Upon her death, her anger is still so raw that she disinherited her children. As an adult woman, years later, I recognized a broken and abused woman who was simply doing what she knew to survive. As a broken, abused teenager, I needed so much more. She could not leave her husband and convinced me that, as a Christian, it was my duty not to prosecute my father. Forgiveness was expected as well as my silence from this point forward. The police begged me to testify, but my guilty soul wouldn't allow me. My mother had convinced me that, somehow, I must have provoked my father's advances and probably made more out of it than was actually true. She assured me if I kept my silence I would be protected and forgiven for attempting to ruin our family's reputation. It wasn't said in those exact words, but that is what was implied, and that is what I walked down the aisle to a year later.

Because I always like to share hope, I want to take this opportunity to share that before my beloved mother passed, we were reconciled. Facing death can, in my understanding. cause one to open their eyes and heart. I had the opportunity to be a caregiver for my mother for a short while after her time in the ICU. In my humble opinion, it was another divinely appointed time. I believe it was about the second night of little to no sleep, on my air mattress at the foot of my mother's bed that I was awakened to crying and what I thought was a need for something. I couldn't imagine what was so important at 2 AM, and I do remember complaining to my mother that if I could not get to sleep, I wouldn't be able to properly care for her the next day. She burst into tears, and I immediately sprang to her side. I felt awful, and she was inconsolable. What was happening? My mother looked up and begged for my forgiveness. "What?! Of course, I forgive you, but for what?"

We spent the next few hours talking, crying, confessing and forgiving one another. Because of our reconciliation, as an adult, a mom and fellow survivor, I have been able to forgive and look back to see silver linings. In her last three years, my mother truly attempted to be loving. For this, I am eternally grateful. Many years later, I wrote a piece for one of my classes entitled the Metamorphosis of Fango Femina (the Broken Woman.) The woman rode in a long black train of despair. In the story, there were tales of how she had come to be on this train, but after so many years, it mattered less and less as to why - only how she would ever be able to get off. The depths of her despair were as firmly rooted as the buried tentacles of an ancient Sequoia. One day, God, disguised as a young scholar, boards the train. From a distance, at first yet always within sight, His peaceful aura was like a beacon of light drawing Fango Femina closer and closer. She was eventually transformed, as a caterpillar transformed into a butterfly. Because of her metamorphosis she was finally able to disembark, and it was witnessed by all aboard the Train of Transformation. I am so grateful this was part of my mother's story as well as mine. Maybe it can be a part of yours.

During the next year, I decided to cement my shaky relationship with my boyfriend. Despite our vows of purity, we let our hormones rule the night after a school dance. Of course, we had to be the 1% who got pregnant after their first time. After an altercation with an unsafe bumper car, I lost the unborn child, which, after years of reflection, I felt was for the best. Teenage pregnancy can be difficult enough, but with no husband, no job, no education and too often judgmental family and society, young parents can really have it rough. This was not how I imagined my new life starting. The engagement was on and off. Then, at Thanksgiving after witnessing his graduation from basic training, it was decided a Christmas wedding was going to happen. All so we could begin our new lives together in England, the first stop on his military orders. Four weeks had to be enough time to plan our nuptials. This would be my final time running away, and, in my mind, it could not happen soon enough.

Once again, after much introspection, this marriage was doomed from the beginning. We both came in with so much baggage. Our families wanted nothing to do with one another and were so disappointed in our choice of spouse. I would describe our time in England for four years as a long honeymoon. We spent three short months in San Antonio, Texas, 37 days of leave, then a first-class flight across the pond. I am pretty sure we both feel this was the best time of our marriage. No families to intrude, just enough money to pay the bills and travel, and we learned and grew in all aspects of our lives. No real responsibility, no kids, and even when things weren't perfect, we both chose to make the next day a better day. We worked at the base chapel and ran youth ministries for both high school and middle school. To this day, I still have a beloved portrait hanging on my walls of these kids. Helping others is a truly powerful experience.

One of the most rewarding experiences was getting to host our Deployed Dependents Dinners. Once a month, during Desert Storm, we invited the spouses of those deployed to enjoy a steak dinner, some time off from kids and fellowship with celebrities. Athletes, Singers, Movie Stars, whomever we could get to come, hang out with them and give them some encouragement. This led to also being on the crew who brought

Bob Hope over for his very last USO Show! Latoya Jackson, Brook Shields and Rosemary Clooney were just some of the celebrities who participated. For this and other work with the Chapel, I was put up for the Angel Award. I also got to have lunch with then Vice President, Dan Quayle, and Bob Hope. This was an amazing opportunity.

Reality came crashing down in the form of an early discharge from the Air Force. There was some sort of security breach. Although they couldn't pin it on my husband, he was asked to take an early discharge. It would not be considered dishonorable but simply as an early administrative discharge. I wanted him to fight it, but he just wanted to go home. So, that's what we did. I believe this was, for me, the beginning of the end of my confidence in my partner. Fair or not, there it was.

Upon returning home, despite misgivings and the fact that Orange County was going bankrupt, we returned to our original roots. We began going back to school, working multiple jobs and simply trying to keep our heads above water. Our families disliked one another no less, and then came the Big News! I thought I had the flu, but no, God was laughing at me... I was pregnant. I remember telling the nurse to go back and find another test result because that couldn't be mine. I convinced my partner we were not capable of being parents. Neither of us had any good examples of what healthy parenting looked like, so we should simply give the child up for adoption.

Crazily enough, this was my third pregnancy. I had suffered from an ectopic pregnancy right after we were married. Since I do not believe in abortion, I carried the child until my fallopian tube burst, and I almost hemorrhaged to death. I felt, at the time, that with the two previous losses, maybe it was some kind of sign from God that motherhood was not for me. Obviously, I later had a change of heart. After rumination, about halfway through, God and I decided that we were going to tackle this thing called Motherhood. Holding my adorable first son, I was hooked. He was so precious and tiny, well tiny is relative, right? He was a huge bouncing, almost ten-pound bundle of joy! I knew it would not be easy, but most of my life hadn't been easy. Maybe I could use some of that tenacity and stubbornness to tackle parenting.

We had been invited to Colorado for Christmas. This was my husband's father and stepmom. I barely knew them, but after my grandmother's death, California was no longer the safest place to raise a little one. So, we chose to move. We landed in Loveland, and it was lovely. My husband, his parents and the Lutheran church pretty much raised my son, as I knew they were all more qualified than I was. I was a workaholic and basically running away once again, not that I would ever have admitted that.

I owned a few businesses, taught Sunday School and was active in the community. You would have thought my life was perfect. My second son came along. I tried to be a bit more involved this time around, but my youngest son was constantly sick and seemed to be allergic to everything but air. No perfumes, dyes, chemicals, and even baby formula made him vomit or break out in hives. He had the RSV virus, asthma and was allergic to trees, grass, and so much more.

Other than that, as I stated above, my life seemed idyllic. Looking back, I can see there was a distance growing between myself and Prince Charming, but nothing I felt that was insurmountable. One day, my partner and I were arguing, and I recall responding with, "Don't you love me?" His response was, "No!" I stopped dead in my tracks. What? Okay, well I guess that makes things different. We did give counseling a try, attempted to have the church help out as well as his family, but he had already decided he was leaving. With a job promotion in another state, he did exactly that. Throughout this time, I learned many things about my husband and myself. I could use this time to recount all of our sins, but I will not. I was still a people pleaser, he was struggling to be his own man and neither of us truly understood healthy boundaries or how to budget. Finances were a huge mess. Romance was the stuff of the past, and I never truly acknowledged until years later that there was so much baggage and trauma in our marriage bed that I never felt safe or loved. Suffice it to say, we each had our issues and had been ignoring them for some time.

I think everyone assumed the boys would return to my family. Although I did consider it briefly, I decided it was definitely not for the best. When I chose to leave my family, it was not an easy decision but one to this day I am grateful I made. Setting these types of boundaries is beyond difficult, but I wanted and desired a different lifestyle. I didn't feel my adopted family could help me in this area, so I chose to move forward without them. That comes at a cost. One you cannot fully account for at the moment but will have lasting consequences if you choose to keep that healthy boundary in place.

For me this meant struggling financially, truly being on my own and sometimes lonely. I was not feeling safe and secure with all the unknowns, but in hindsight, it was worth it. Today, I have restored some of those relationships, but only those in which I felt safe, respected and loved. I am grateful to have been able to restore and keep some of my childhood friendships and maintain some connections with women, counselors and teachers who were able to help me along my journey. Because of the choices I have made, I have experienced wealth, poverty, disability, chronic illness, joy and peace. Each has a place within my story.

I had been in the hospitality industry my whole life and decided this was not the most reliable industry for a single mother. I ventured into the financial industry and became consumed with perfection once again. I learned I was good at sales and loved helping folks keep their money safe. I began going out almost every weekend and working astronomical hours. The boys spent more time with my ex's family and in childcare than with me, but in my mind, this was for the best. I was not Betty Crocker, June Cleaver or Carol Brady. The boys were young but have since shared that they hated this particular time of their lives. As a mother, I feel horrible. I was not there for them as I should have been. I remember one summer evening, the windows were all open, the boys were misbehaving, and I was at the end of my short rope. I was yelling, and after swatting their behinds and putting them to bed early, there was a knock on the door. The police had received a call, because a neighbor was worried abuse might be taking place. My boys told the nice police officers that they had been not listening and nothing was wrong. They were sorry, and no abuse was evident. The officers let me know that a social worker would contact me soon, and maybe I should consider lowering my voice. Wow! The social worker and I had a pleasant enough visit, and I admitted I had no idea what I was doing, but I loved my sons and asked if there was such a thing as a class on parenting. She assured me there was help if I was open to it and agreed with the officers that there were no signs of abuse or neglect and wished me the best. She gave me some books to read, set me up with a parenting class and left us alone. It was my wakeup call as a mother. I did not want to become my mother. I read every book on parenting I could get my hands on, went to classes offered and moved my sons back close to my ex's family. I was never going to be the perfect TV mom, but I was much more invested, and the boys and I began to grow closer. We were nurturing one another and became a beautiful little family unit. My little saplings were being enriched, and we were all reaching for much-needed sunlight, just like my Sequoia was still doing in its new home within the National Forest.

This is another good place to share some cool perspectives on what nurturing looks like when you're not the perfect tv mom. For me, I have been given so many opportunities through my education late in life to reflect on a myriad of topics, and my sons were often the main topic of my papers. As they are the center of my world outside of my relationship with God, this is not surprising. One class in particular, Virgil and the Latin Golden Age with Professor Bubb, I was challenged to reflect on ancient literature and to put it into practice or reflection in my daily life. As a single mother of two sons, I could not help but be drawn to the tale of Phaethon. Because their earthly father is too often absent, these siblings plead with their Heavenly Father for unrealistic desires. They immaturely lust after deeds filled with glory and honor before they are ready. Inevitably they and all they love are plunged into darkness. Praise God our story is a bit different.

My sons definitely pushed boundaries and sought after all kinds of things. Knowing I was lacking in an ability to set healthy boundaries and never wanting to be considered abusive, I sought help. I desired for my sons to climb mountains and slay dragons...these are rites of passage into manhood, but I desired them to be properly trained beforehand. So, I asked the healthy men in my life to be their mentors. I prayed over this for days and months and sought out safe, trustworthy men of character, and God provided. Dallas, Tim, Ryan, Isaac and, later, Brian were the most amazing mentors, adopted Uncles and Giant Sequoias in my sons' lives. Honest to goodness, these brothers in the faith restored my trust and allowed me to begin seeing that men could be healthy, honest and loving. So much so, that when it came time for me to hire a caregiver, allow a physical therapist into my personal space and engage with a mental health professional, I sought out other men who continued to nurture me and meet me where I was at.

God is so amazing when we will let Him work in our lives. He truly transforms us from spaces of fear, mistrust and bitterness to spaces rich and full of silver linings and unconditional love. I would like to add that raising boys or young men definitely had its challenges for me. As you can imagine, many of my relationships with men were less than ideal and challenging at best. It has been asked of me, how exactly did I manage this? Suffice it to say, that for me, my sons represented an opportunity to break cycles and patterns within my own past but also the future relationships my sons might one day encounter. I raised them with unconditional love, respect and grace. I sought help from other men who I witnessed were healthy and engaging in being loving men to their wives, mothers, friends and others in their communities. I read every book I could get my hands on regarding building up young men and shaping them to be not only productive but highly emotionally intelligent. Here is a small list of some of the books I found helpful:

- *Parenting With Love and* [21].
- *The 5 Love Languages of* [22]
- *Wild Things: The Art of Nurturing Boys*[23]
- *Do Hard Things* [24]
- *The Resolution for Men*[25]

We watched movies and discussed how they might want to model themselves after courageous and trustworthy characters. We explored music of many genres so as to connect on an emotional and cerebral level. We conversed as transparently and vulnerably as possible at different stages of their lives. I never tried to hide who we were or where we came from or where we hoped to go together and separately. I encouraged my sons to be independent yet strongly connected with family. I am not saying I was perfect in all these teachings and in my guidance. However, unconditional love was at the heart of all I attempted to show my sons, and to this day, it is the one thing both my sons thanked me for accomplishing.

During my writing and research for this book I came across some facts which I think are important to share. Many years ago, I read a book entitled *Trauma Through a Child's Eyes* by Peter A. Levine and Maggie Kline. It was staggering to read all the statistics they shared about partners and their children who had dealt with domestic violence within their homes. Simply witnessing and surviving these awful circumstances affected their eating habits, their sleep, their emotions and so much more. 75% of children from violent homes are physically and sexually abused[26]. They are 20 times more likely to become perpetrators themselves, especially boys.[27] Unfortunately, only about 25% of those affected will seek professional help.[28] My boys and I are grateful to be a part of the latter percentage, and we built relationships so that we could be true cycle breakers. Sometimes when we are young, unprotected and faced with physical fears, threats, abuse etc... we can be removed, but we will still have the fear embedded in our head and hearts. The fears can be seared into our very souls. This, in turn, brands and shapes our personalities. It can corral our spirits into a smaller space than it is used to living in. We might see danger in places where none exist. Then, when we come to our Creator, we do so defensively and full of mistrust. God wants us to return to our childhood and learn to trust Him, run to Him as a child would to a loving parent. He desires for us to come to an understanding that He is a Father who can be trusted. As children who have been hurt and abused, we lose confidence in loved ones who should have protected us. As a result, our internal rules change. We may develop an internal fort where we will be the soul gatekeeper. Years pass, and the walls become more impenetrable. We may even lose the key. There are many who perhaps understand this. Usually, it will take a defining moment or event within our walk with the Lord. It may take years for us to turn to God when we are afraid, but the key is to never stop walking with God. My desire through sharing all this is to help myself and others to turn to God rather than ourselves when we are afraid. When we are overwhelmed, we want to learn to open the door rather than close it. Then our Heavenly Father, who truly does have great plans for us, can easily walk through.

On the journey with my tribe

---

[20] Larcom, L. (1893). *Plant a tree*. In *Poems* (public domain). https://poemanalysis.com/lucy-larcom/plant-a-tree/

[21] Cline, F., & Fay, J. (2006). *Parenting with love and logic: Teaching children responsibility* (Updated ed.). NavPress.

[22]Chapman, G. D., & Campbell, R. (2016). *The 5 love languages of children: The secret to loving children effectively* (3rd ed.). Northfield Publishing. https://www.amazon.com/Love-Languages-Children-Secret-Effectively/dp/0802412858

[23] James, S., & Thomas, D. (2009). *Wild things: The art of nurturing boys*. Tyndale House Publishers.

[24] Harris, A., & Harris, B. (2008). *Do hard things: A teenage rebellion against low expectations*. Multnomah Books. https://www.penguinrandomhouse.com/books/75598/do-hard-things-by-alex-harris-and-brett-harris/9781601428295/

[25]Kendrick, S., & Kendrick, A. (2011). *The resolution for men*. B&H Books. https://www.amazon.com/Resolution-Men-Stephen-Kendrick/dp/1433671220

[26] Levine, P. A., & Kline, M. (2007). *Trauma through a child's eyes: Awakening the ordinary miracle of healing*. North Atlantic Books

[27] Levine, P. A., & Kline, M. (2007). *Trauma through a child's eyes: Awakening the ordinary miracle of healing*. North Atlantic Books

[28]Levine, P. A., & Kline, M. (2007). *Trauma through a child's eyes: Awakening the ordinary miracle of healing*. North Atlantic Books

"Trees give peace to the soul..."
Nora Wain[29]

Chapter Seven

You might think, as I did, that my happily ever after was on the horizon. I deserved some peace, some rest, and my drama was going to be enjoyed on a stage rather than in my daily minutia. I was losing weight, still not really sleeping but that would come; I was sure of it. I wrote in my journal and tried my best to be there for my sons who had become my whole world. I wore so many masks, because there were so many people to please and my weight loss was not because I was engaging in healthier eating. I was binging and purging on a daily basis now. If I didn't have a body to please a husband then I would get one - even if it killed me.

If I overwhelmed others with my confidence and abilities, then I would kill them with kindness - even if it meant no longer meeting my own personal needs. If the boys needed anything, I would drop everything to make it happen - even, especially if it was inconvenient, because their needs superseded mine. None of these unrealistic, people-pleasing methods were placed on me by anyone but myself. Psychology helps you, and I understand this is part of a learned coping mechanism. In my mind I was trying to earn my way in this world. I thought that if I just worked harder, then, surely, I could please someone. Surely, I could be found worthy of love.

During this time, my birthday rolled around, and I thought I really needed a night out. None of my regular friends were available, but this one girl from work said she would go out dancing with me. Up to this point in my life, I have always been smart and safe when going out. I barely knew this girl, and we hadn't set up any safe boundaries and basically, I was alone. I was so alone, and unknowingly in danger, but recklessly proceeded to celebrate like there was no tomorrow. God and I were not on the best of terms at that time, and I was tired of being the 'good girl' and always feeling like a disappointment. What had being safe gotten me? Nothing! I do not remember how many drinks I had that night or how long I had been on the dance floor. One of those drinks was spiked with Rohypnol, and I ended up leaving with a complete stranger. Something I had never done before. He took me back to his place, and he and his five friends had their way with me for several hours. I woke up several hours later, and I was so ashamed. How could I have let this happen? What kind of mother was this irresponsible? I found my way out to my car, crawled behind the wheel and found myself sitting on the side of the road.

My thoughts were so dark at this point that I am not exactly sure how it happened, but I pulled out in front of a huge Mac truck hoping it would run me over. The driver swerved and just missed me. Sigh, the driver was naturally furious with me, and I apologized and headed home. Luckily, the boys were being watched overnight. I took a shower, began to drink coffee and decided I should probably get some help. I called my pastor who

I had not spoken with in months, and he responded with grace. He suggested calling the police and committed to sending me some names of counselors he thought might be able to help. Of course, I had already taken a shower, but they processed a rape kit anyway. Rohypnol showed up in my blood work, and there were obvious signs of forced sex. All that was in my favor.

When the case went to trial, it didn't stand up in court. My rapist got away. This was truly discouraging, and I would like to pause for a minute to reflect back on some of my misplaced guilt and trauma after surviving a rape. Going out is not bad; choosing to let your hair down is not bad. Getting raped is always the rapist's responsibility, never the victims'. It doesn't matter how many drinks, how short the skirt was or what the make-up looked like. My rapist eventually got caught and served time for his crimes. My voice did help in building a case against him. With my silver lining in all of this, I found my first good counselor who helped me begin to start on a path of healing. I felt like, for the first time, I might be on the right footing. Someone was not only listening to me but helping me to see how broken I truly was.

Finding my voice in the forest

[29] Waln, N. (n.d.). *Trees give peace to the souls of men.*

"The trees that are slow to grow bear the best fruit."
Moliere[30]

Chapter Eight

All's well that ends well, but this is just intermission. The beginning of the second act is upcoming, and it promises to be eventful to say the least. During this fragile time of healing, I met John Wayne reincarnated...truly that was my description to friends and family. My counselor tried to get me to go slow and gave me her professional opinion that I was not ready, but I wasn't listening. Besides, my boys could use an active, loving stepfather. I was lonely, and my cowboy was pretty perfect. After a whirlwind romance, we were engaged then married in under a year.

About three months into my new happily ever after, we had a disagreement of some kind. I honestly don't remember exactly what it was about, but what I do remember is him throwing the keys so hard they were embedded in the wall behind my head. They had just missed me by inches. I was shaking, and I ran out of the house trying to catch my breath. My cowboy assured me he didn't know what came over him, and he was terribly sorry he had scared me. Please forgive him, and he promised it would never happen again. Except, in less than a few weeks, something even worse happened. This time, he backhanded me for some slight and disrespect on my part. My cowboy hugged me so tight afterwards and soothed me until I stopped crying. Once again, he assured me it wouldn't happen again. Some of you know how this ends, but I truly thought it would all be fine, and for some strange reason it, must be me.

In my mind, I could deal with a husband who had a bit of a temper as long as my boys were doing well and he was such a good father. Oh, how wrong I was, but a good abuser never lets the right hand know what the left is doing. And an even better manipulator always has the weaker partner believing it is their fault. I didn't know at the time what gaslighting was, but I was buried in it. The abuse continued and moved into some dark places in the bedroom and began to permeate every aspect of my life. The cowboy was in complete control by this point, and I was a willing captive. I had a business which failed, and we had to move. So, the cowboy moved us back to his hometown, which I was hopeful of might be a great opportunity for change. My youngest was still having health issues, and a new environment might be exactly what the doctor ordered.

The tiny hometown we moved to was so remote and only served to make all of us more susceptible to our cowboy's need for total control. I remember sitting on the bleachers, and the Sheriff, (who happened to be the cowboy's second cousin), settled down next to me. He calmly, without looking at me, said softly that I should consider learning not to piss him off, him being the cowboy. I knew at that moment I was totally alone, and there was no one to help me. I remember crying that night into my pillow and crying out to God. By this point, I felt like I surely must have been created to be abused. I did my best daily to not upset my cowboy, but it was like walking on eggshells. You never knew who was going to come through the door, therefore, pleasing him was not always possible. In my mind, it was all worth it if the boys were well, and as far as I knew they were.

I remember the first crack in my defenses came from a good friend. She showed up, claimed to know what was going on and told me she was prepared to help. I, of course, denied everything, but she would not accept it. I told her, even if she was correct, cowboy was never going to just let us go. He would kill us first. She asked me to let her and her husband help and asked me to be patient. Thank goodness for her tenacity. She never dropped it and spoke with me often about plans of escape. I was slowly softening, and my eyes were being opened. I came home early one day and, unexpectedly, my cowboy was home early. No one heard me enter. Thus, as I heard yelling and wandered into the kitchen, I was shocked to see cowboy kicking my youngest across the floor. I went berserk and jumped on his back and started hitting him. My youngest ran from the room, and I paid for my courage. He beat me soundly, but my eyes were officially open. I realized my boys were not safe. I called my friend, and it took us a few months, but we began to plan for our escape.

The plan was to leave on Valentine's Day. I had used the last couple months to store away antiques, special family heirlooms, paintings and photo albums. I rented a storage unit in a neighboring town in my mother's maiden name, and I got good at lying about where things went. Every chance I got, I squirreled away every penny I could. I was able to amass a whole $3,000, but it was better than nothing. I called a few folks previously in my life but far, far away. I shared a few details and asked for help.

Amazingly, one of the people who came through was the boys' father. He didn't judge and genuinely wanted to help. With my permission, he proceeded to contact his parents, under strict orders, that *no one* could speak of what we were considering.

Unbeknownst to anyone, his parents had bought a beautiful home on a lake in the Pacific Northwest. They mailed keys, MapQuest directions (yes, it was the early 2000s, and that's how we knew where we were going) and about $300 for gas. The night before, we went to a friend's house to play cards, and my friend's husband messed with my cowboy's truck so it wouldn't start in the morning. Totally unseen to an amateur mechanic. I don't know what possessed me, but we had a huge argument that night, and, as I was begging for forgiveness and asking if maybe we could attempt counseling (we obviously needed help), cowboy walked over to the gun cabinet, pulled out his shotgun, threw the phone at me and dared me to dial 9-1-1. He assured me I would not get there fast enough. I placed the phone back on its base, kissed him on the cheek, and proceeded to bed where I knew what would be coming, but I was willing to take it for one last night. He fell asleep quickly after he got his needs met, but I was awake for several hours before I fell into a fitful sleep.

I was so exhausted I barely felt him leave, but I was awakened shortly to yelling and cursing and a demand I get up immediately to take him to work as his truck wasn't starting. I think I might have been up for actress of the year as I feigned surprise and frustration at having to drive him all the way out to his worksite. On the way there, I reminded him that I had special plans for us for Valentine's Day and could he please ask one of the guys to bring him home. I wanted everything to be extra special and assured him we would have the whole night to ourselves as his parents were watching the boys. He grumbled but quickly said yes, as he was anticipating an entire evening of getting to play master with his servant. I am sure he could not wait.

During this time, I had also gotten two important things in my name only. A car for my business and a Motorola cell phone. After his speedy departure, I immediately called my friend so she and her husband could meet me back at the house. I got the boys off to school and went to three close friends who I swore to secrecy, and they agreed to help us out. We filled three cars full of stuff and drove it to my storage unit. We came back and filled my little Isuzu Trooper to the hilt, leaving just enough space for the boys. I rehomed my cat, gave away clothes and keepsakes to my friends who helped us out, cleared all legal documents, phone memory and computer logs, etc., basically trying to erase any info and existence of me and the boys. I wanted us to be able to fall off the face of the earth with little to no trace.

I cried, gave hugs and went to pick up the boys from school. The boys crawled into the car and wondered what was going on. I told them I was moving stuff into my work storage unit and not to worry about it. Get out your homework, and we will grab a snack on the road. I took off for the state line, and once we made it into the neighboring state, I pulled over to let the boys know, through my tears, that we would not be returning - ever. They, of course, had a million questions, were scared about what the future would hold and concerned for their friends and our family we were leaving. By the time we got to our first hotel, after prayer and many more tears, I watched the boys fall into a fitful sleep. I finally was able to close my eyes and catch a few winks. We decided a swim would be in order, hit the pool and had a late breakfast. The first full day on the road was pretty silent. I don't think any of us knew what to say. That night, after the boys fell asleep, I checked in with my friends. They actually shared as little as possible, because my focus needed to be on reaching our destination and not worrying about cowboy or anyone else. The third night found us in Pocatello with two new beds and a coffee machine.

Right before publishing this story, I was given the most serendipitous opportunity. On a recent trip back to Washington, I had the chance to stay in Pocatello, ID at the exact hotel the boys and I had stayed at while running for our very lives. I observed a mother and her sons in the breakfast room, I walked around the pool we had swam in and slept in a room with two beds and a coffee machine. I shed a few tears, but they were tears of joy and filled with a huge sense of triumph. It was 20 years, and I was now living a new life with new hopes and dreams, and I had overcome it all in every way possible.

Finding joy

[30] Molière. (1673/ n.d.). *The imaginary invalid. (Original work published 1673)*

"There's nothing wrong with having a tree as a friend."
Bob Ross[31]

Chapter Nine

Because I like to find my silver linings, I feel it's an appropriate time to share just some of the many blessings which happened over the next few years. We couldn't have found a better place to land than this fantastic area of the Pacific Northwest. The YWCA, Marines for Tots, P.E.O. - a loving fantastic group of women, The Salvation Army, two amazing Community Colleges, my beloved Alma Mater, Gonzaga University, Christ Kitchen, and the list could truly go on forever. These agencies were all there for the boys and I in more ways than we could ever imagine. As well as my church family, friends and our later Marine Family. As I am a teacher and life coach at heart, I want to point out a few things here. Folks who pray together stay together. I do not know who first coined that phrase, but I have found it to be true. And nowhere was this more evident than with my Marine Family. Have I previously mentioned that my family loves to serve? Grandfathers, Dads, Uncles, brothers, cousins, the boy's father, and finally my eldest son. We have had at least one person in each generation for more than five generations who have signed on the dotted line, sworn their oaths and served in every branch except the Coast Guard.

My son chose the Marines, but we parents like to say we were drafted. Of all my military experiences, I found this one particularly difficult. I am a self-professed control freak, and, in this scenario, it was made clear I had no control. Your son or daughter chooses this, and you support it or don't. Either way, they have chosen. Similar to having a parent serve, as a military brat, you have no choice in where you move, the crazy long hours and the deployments. But as a parent, I think you have even less control, but now after surviving the raising of another human being where you had control and held all responsibility, you have no control. You, the parents, are asked to give that all up willingly, so the Military can break them down and turn them into Marines. Don't take this wrong. I totally understand the importance of children leaving home and becoming independent, but there is something about your child being asked to possibly give their life while they still can't legally drink, rent a car, or gamble. Heck, they just became old enough to vote for their Commander-In-Chief. Their frontal lobes are not even fully developed. So, as a parent, this is a whole different level of letting go. You are not a spouse, so you don't have the right to be told much, unless of course they die or are severely injured. You wait for phone calls and texts and anxiously await to see where they are being shipped off to and how long this deployment or training will last. I remember a particular call from my son in which he awkwardly asked if I could be his person who was notified if he should not return. I laughed with my son and heartily assured him I was his person, then upon hanging up, I cried my eyes out. I was a parent who thankfully never received that phone call, but I know too many who did. So, your Marine Family, or my Bravo Family as they have been affectionately known since we banded together, are some of the greatest Sequoias in my life. Several of us, even years after our son's time of service was long over, are still praying together daily. That is the purest definition of family. A circle which shall never be broken.

The boys and I were able to stay pretty much off the grid, no bills in our names, no bank accounts, cell phones set for complete emergencies, escape plans. Simply naming a few of these places makes me nervous. We did everything we could to be safe and remain safe. Cowboy definitely tried to find us. We had school records sent to three different locations before finding their way to us. Doctors, therapists and schools were all vigilant with us, and everyone worked together to keep us safe. Even when we first ventured onto social media, everything was locked down pretty tight. I remember the first time I forgot and was on Instagram publicly for a role within my church family, and cowboy found me. Not literally thank goodness, but online, and he sent me some nasty messages. We shut that down and got new phones and were extra vigilant once again.

So, why am I talking as freely as I am at this moment? Well, it's not easy, but I am in a very different place in my life right now. I don't know if this is my wisest choice, but I also know I am no longer willing to live in fear. I am choosing to speak up, as my story, my transparency and my vulnerability may help someone else. I also know I am no longer the victim, the broken woman, the needy little girl who just wants to be loved. I am loved, I am confident, I am enough and God is with me. So, I choose not to be silent any longer. I am still always trying to be safe and discerning in my choices; however, that is different than hiding. I don't share my personal address and phone number with just anyone. I still screen and weed out strangers, whether it's via phone or social media. I have been told this is actually pretty normal even for folks who haven't been through what I have, so I feel good about what I am doing now: living richly and fully, yet mindfully.

As is my way, and as I remember different times throughout this journey, I feel the need to bring up another important part of my Tribe. While at Gonzaga, I found myself once again becoming unlikely friends with another professor. Anne and I didn't hit it off right away, as seems to be the way with me. However, once again, by the end of the term, we went to coffee and became lifelong friends. She invited me into this beautiful, ecumenical book club. I met some of the most amazing women, many who are still lifelong friends. I also had several professors who made such an impact that my time at Gonzaga will remain one of my favorite parts of my story. I describe these parts of my desired family as being part of my Tribe. Each person has a special place in my heart and my story.

One more very important part of my Tribe is my little sister, not by blood but by faith, in my heart and by my side for more than a decade now. EJ, or Erin to me, came into my life when she was studying the Bible before choosing to dedicate her life to Christ and be baptized. It was such an honor to walk with her through this process, and it cemented our relationship for all eternity. We have been roommates, caregiver and client, business partners and besties. She is the little sister I always dreamed of. I mention EJ and all these others, because I truly want you to know I was never alone! I did not survive and learned to thrive in a vacuum. My life has been filled with the most amazing friends and family, and I am blessed to be a part of an amazing community.

Silver linings

---

[31] Ross, B. (n.d.). *There's nothing wrong with having a tree as a friend.*

"Stand strong, firm and rooted like a solid tree. Though distractions may cause you to waiver, remain balanced and calm."

Leigh Hershkovich[32]

Chapter Ten

Back to the bedside of the broken woman who had a stroke of unknown origins. I had by now tried to end my life twice, once by Mack Truck and now through overdosing on my insulin. My A1C, which is a three-month barometer, if you will, for gauging how well you are managing your diabetes, was at a 12. For those who don't know, this is a staggering number. Pre-diabetics are usually around six. I have been suffering from some bouts of hepatic encephalopathy, which is brain fog and toxins building up in your system (which can lead to comas) off and on over the last few years. I was considered morbidly obese and weighed about 360 pounds at just 5' 3" tall.

A good friend, while sitting by my bed, spoke with me frankly and honestly and shared with me that he had just realized that I didn't love myself. I think I laughed and cried my response. Since when was loving yourself a requirement for healthy living? He assured me that if I did not know how to love myself, I could not possibly truly understand how to love others. I was hurt, horrified and in shock. What had I been doing all these years if

I hadn't been loving others? He hugged me and assured me that through Christ all things are possible, that I had been sharing Christ's love with others. But on a personal level, within my inner circle and definitely within my own heart and mind, I had most probably been lost at sea for some time, rudderless if you will. However, if I could learn to put on my own oxygen mask, fill up my cup and value my creation, I could find peace, love, trust and finally seize the Hope I was so desperately seeking.

It sounded so easy. HAHAHA! He definitely encouraged me to seek out a good counselor, as he was one but couldn't be mine, professional boundaries and all being what they are. And, had I considered losing weight? I froze! As you may or may not have guessed, my weight had become my false security blanket, and I would rather walk through a vat of acid than lose it. I told him exactly that, and he challenged me to pray about it and bring it up with my doctor and my future counselor. I mumbled something that sounded like a yes, but I don't think I really intended to follow through with it, at least not at this point. This was simply too much, and I honestly did not believe I could do it. By the time I had a conversation with my next amazing therapist, I was simply ready to be finished with this race. She and I worked on getting my nightmares under control, so I could get some rest. I took some meds traditionally given to PTSD veterans, which, for simplicity's sake, stopped my dreams. It was a little slice of heaven to be able to close my eyes and not be harassed by the terrors of the night. We re-worked my will, because I was preparing for death or, at least in my mind, coming to terms with its inevitableness. I was able to find some peace, but we still had not dug into some of the really tough stuff. We tried some EMDR, which was difficult for me to say the least. In the middle of it, I suffered a second, mini stroke. This one was physically from the waist down and slightly delayed my speech and cognitive function. The mind is a powerful thing, and my physical shell was still very unhealthy. My counselor asked me if I had ever considered bariatric surgery? Yes, I had a few years back, but I failed the psychological examination - ok, my terminology, but the results were the same. The psychologist felt that, at that time, I would most likely sabotage any good results, and none of my labs were good either. They suggested I seek counseling and come back when I was ready. I promptly decided it was for the best, went home, then binged on some ice cream and wine. I fell back into my unhealthy eating habits, once again, because it was the easiest. I also wasn't ready to give up my security blanket anyway. So, my current counselor asked me if I might be ready. We had come so far, and maybe I was ready to tackle this next challenge. As things happen, she left St Luke's not long after, but she had sparked in me the same thought as my friend. If I loved myself and what God created, then maybe I should find a way to take care of my body/my temple and engage in some self-care and self-love. Besides, by this time in my journey I had four beautiful grandchildren, and there seemed to be a lot to live for.

I plucked up the courage to speak with my primary doctor, and she thought bariatric surgery could be something really good for me. We also knew at this point that my poor health and dying liver were not going to help me on this journey. There would be many costs to count. I can't tell you I went to the first appointment with the Bariatric team full of enthusiasm or confidence, but I was carrying some faith and hope with me. I spoke with a nurse and a nutritionist who gave me an overwhelming amount of information, but I was determined to keep putting one foot in front of the other. I even made an appointment for my psychological review. I was attempting to follow the nutritional advice and losing a little weight. I couldn't do a ton of physical exercise at this point, but I was committed to walking and had begun dancing in my home. Dancing is a loose term I use but moving to the beat of some oldies-but-goodies and trying not to end up on the floor is probably more accurate. The YouTube instructor assured me no one was watching and to go at my own pace; I literally laughed out loud but kept moving.

The day the psychologist's appointment came, I was so nervous I almost threw up, but I was determined to keep moving forward with this process. I had journaled and prayed about this; I decided that honesty and transparency were my best choices and spoke as simply and plainly as possible. Afterwards, she didn't judge me; she actually seemed to empathize with me and assured me I was not alone. She said she was going to recommend I be allowed to move forward in this pursuit, but that steady counseling would really be necessary if I truly wanted this to work. She was rightly concerned I would fall easily back into self-sabotaging habits if I was not intentional and mindful. She thought she knew just the person I should see. It was a man. She immediately assured me she had heard my story and knew I would have reservations, but she was confident that if I gave him a chance, I might be pleasantly surprised. She also told me that if it didn't work out to ask her for another referral. In no way could I imagine how this was going to work out or be a good thing, but I was committed to moving forward. So, I found myself sitting in Anthony's office a few weeks later.

Once again, I prayed and journaled and kept walking and dancing and following my nutritional guidelines and, knowing I could ask for a different counselor, I followed through and showed up. I seriously do not remember exactly what I shared in that first appointment, but never did I feel judged, never did I feel uncomfortable or scared. Anthony was calm, polite and insightful. At times, too insightful; I felt like he could see right through me but in a challenging and helpful way. He didn't shy away from the tough questions, and he didn't let me either. It was exactly what I needed, and it was a man. Okay God, I am listening. Maybe I could have a professional, healthy relationship with a guy... maybe. Let's just see where this goes and, in the meantime, I will keep putting one foot in front of the other. My surgeon was a man, too, and as luck would have it, the original surgeon who had discovered my liver disease. Can you imagine my surprise and his? We remembered one another, and he explained to me why he moved to bariatrics from general surgery. He wanted to help his patients before they were so sick that he was seeing them for emergency surgeries. We discussed the fact that my liver disease truly complicated this whole bariatric process, but the rest of my lab work was looking great. I had truly worked to get my diabetes under control and was now sitting at an A1C of seven. I had given up diet soda completely, had lost around 20 pounds by this time and was sticking to my nutritionist's advice. I was ready. He did want me to have a frank discussion with my sons regarding the possibility of my dying during this procedure. He typically didn't do surgery on patients with my level of poor health. I could not do the full bypass, which is the gold standard in weight loss surgery, but he felt we could do the sleeve. I was slightly disappointed at first, because I wanted to give myself the best chance for the most weight loss if I was going to be taking these huge risks. He assured me that the bypass was too dangerous, and with my commitment to the programs afterward and the personal commitments to myself and my family, the sleeve would help me achieve all my healthy goals.

Mentally and emotionally, I tried to focus on new healthy goals. I surrounded myself with people who made me hungry for life, who touched my heart and nourished my soul and I had Anthony, Alex and Meaghan reminding me that these were choices. I was choosing to put this special tool into my toolbox, but I didn't have to do anything if I did not want to. This wasn't some desperate action; it was an appropriate response to my desire to be healthier from the inside out. I had spent most of my life up to this point taking for granted my physical body, or in fear, frustration and anger, abusing it. My MO in life up to this point was to run away from dislikes, stress and confrontations.

Two weeks prior to surgery was a full liquid diet, and that was definitely not fun. If you know me then you know I like drinking coffee, not clear plain, sad water. When it came time for the surgery, I did not want to see another protein shake. Crushing pills was a horrible part of the liquid diet, but it was something my insurance wouldn't cover. It was beyond disgusting and a terrible thing to have to go through. This may sound crazy, but I literally bought baby silverware and baby-sized dishes and storage containers so I didn't have to weigh out two ounces of food. If it fit in my baby-sized jar, then it was about all I ate at one time for several weeks, then I moved up to four ounces at a time. I had little Dixie cups of water measured out and poured, so I didn't drink too much at one time. Also, I knew how to drink so many per hour then none with meals or immediately following meals. Everything was timed and set up for success, and my body let me know immediately if I didn't get it right. Nausea, vomiting and pain could happen quickly, so stay on track or my body would react. Honestly, one of the hardest things was remembering not to drink immediately prior to a meal, during a meal or for 30 minutes following a meal. A huge key seemed to be meal prep, so once it came to the actual eating, it was easy. I just had to decide which two-ounce cup to pull out and partake of. Tiny, small bites taken slowly over 30 minutes, five to six times a day. To relieve stress, I limited social media and news, focusing instead on reading, self-care, family and friends.

At 14 days post-op, I was down about 14 pounds and I was disappointed. Something worth noting is that weight is often a symptom, not the problem. The ugly side of perfectionism rises up quickly, and I really had to journal and pray for a better heart and attitude. God listened and softened my heart and attitude. I needed an attitude adjustment here. Often what we fear the most is exactly what we need. I needed to wrap my head around my fears, embrace them and learn to tolerate the feelings associated with them. I required true transformation within my innermost thoughts, so mistakes, failures and anxieties simply became part of my process. I was learning not to react, rather pay attention and address my feelings and needs. During this healing process, one of the biggest things I learned there was a huge difference between my inner critic and healthy self-reflection. If I have a choice in how I respond, then what happens becomes less important than what I choose to do with it. Feelings are not meant to be controlled, but how we perceive, express and use them is totally within our control. While we can't always change the situation, we can change our thoughts and reactions; this is where our true power lies. So, progress became more important to me than my need for perfection.

I found some journal entries from this time and thought this might be an appropriate place to share some of my processing through this very delicate, emotionally driven time.

4th April

I have the greatest appreciation for food-especially that is prepared for one and not 75 others at the same time. Flavors are richer, juices are flowing, textures are appropriate and not abrasive. It's food heaven. And I don't need a lot-just enough-why can't it be like this forever? I am afraid it will change. Then I ask myself, if I am in charge, why does it have to change? Maybe it doesn't but how do I keep the peace without compromising, without fighting? Are these just natural occurrences that I need to learn to embrace, alongside the joys? I want to move forward boldly in my Faith, knowing nothing is impossible for my God and I. But all I see are questions right now. I am at sea with no land in sight and where normally that would seem adventurous to me, it seems terrifying at this moment. That is beyond unsettling...

18th April

There are many amazing things about this past weekend, but there were some serious lows. It was mentally and emotionally exhausting. I didn't do this weight loss or transformation so I could be anyone's poster child. I don't want that responsibility. Don't get me wrong, I love helping others but need to find my healthy boundaries, and there was a sense throughout this weekend that once again I was wandering back into some unwanted social patterns. I am no one's competition! I might eventually be interested in the possibility of a future relationship, but I don't want to be a trophy, object, or shiny new toy! There is this one sister, who I have tried over and over to please, and once again I seemed to let her down-she reminds me so much of my mother. Albeit a healthier version, yet difficult for me to handle no matter how much I try or how much I pray. I cried. As I look at the weekend overall, I am encouraged. I hoped my new levels of energy would sustain me, and they did. It was amazing to want to do something and simply be able to do so. Most of my other fellowship was so uplifting-truly God blesses me...

Getting off pain meds was amazing; I was less moody. By 16 days post-op I was able to take small leisurely walks. 37 days post-op I was down 30 pounds! I officially cleaned out all my 5x and 6x size clothing and went to my first clothing swap. I am not going to lie; that clothing swap was a huge event for me. In my eyes, I was publicly declaring that not only had I lost weight but that I was never going to return to an unhealthy weight. It was a declaration of great significance. I valued my new body enough to clothe it with apparel that was worthy of its new size.

My weight loss was finally becoming noticeable, and Anthony helped me process all the emotions associated with no longer having the full effect of my false security blanket. I also no longer needed to crush all the pills. My liver enzymes were still much higher than we would have liked, but my diabetic numbers were amazing. At eight weeks, I plateaued for a couple weeks and still hadn't broken the 300 lb. threshold. It was a great time to reevaluate and reflect. Hair loss was another thing no one spoke to me about. It's often a side effect of such a huge surgery and part of our body's reaction to all the changes. I had long, beautiful wavy hair and didn't realize how much a part of my identity and pride it had become until I chose to cut it all off. My hairdresser and I both cried as it was shorn. I did donate more than 12 inches for cancer patients and have since embraced, and begun to enjoy, the short spiky look I chose, but it was definitely difficult.

On the 21st of July, I hit my first big goal of being under 300 pounds - and at my endocrinology appointment I weighed in at 298! Plus, my A1C was 6.1! I hadn't been that low since I was first diagnosed with diabetes. No more insulin; I would begin taking a pill and only having to test a few times a day. This was so huge! I was walking between 2500 - 3000 steps daily. My sleep was more regulated, and I began to dream about what my future might look like. By the end of July, I was down to about 285 but had a nasty reaction to the new diabetic med. Because my body was so sensitive, it put me in the hospital for a few days, but everyone on my health team worked together. I was disappointed to have to temporarily go back to insulin which was easier on my system. I also made a tough decision to let go of one of my long-time caregivers, but she wasn't helping me or meeting me where I desired to be with my new healthy lifestyle. So, I chose someone who had worked for me before, and things were really looking up. I just realized that I haven't, up to this point, made much mention of caregivers before. Once I became eligible for disability, which was a grueling two-year process, it was determined my health was in such a poor state that I qualified for an in-home caregiver. At first, this was simply 30 hours per month, as I had given up my driver's license after passing out behind the wheel with my youngest in the car. The decision to give up driving was difficult, but my doctors and I felt it was a wise choice. As my health worsened, hospital visits increased, then a major neurological event occurred. My need for caregivers became even greater. I wrote a fictional book loosely based on my life, entitled *Carpe Spero.* It explains the fears and intricacies of what having a caregiver means to an independent person. Caregivers can be some of the most amazing parts of a chronic illness journey.

Somewhere along the way, I gained a few pounds and had to process and reevaluate things. Anthony and my tribe never let me fall too far down the rabbit's hole of depression or perfectionism, thank goodness. Then, by the end of November, I found myself 70 pounds down! At my one-year mark, I was down 84 pounds with 26 more to go before I could have my knee replacement surgery... so close. As you can imagine, carrying that much excess weight around for a few decades, my sports-filled youth and simply not caring for my temple had led to bone grinding on bone and the need to have both of my knees replaced with titanium. Climbing stairs, standing for too long, walking any distance and balance had all become a major part of my health concerns.

All of this needed to be addressed if my body was to be transformed physically. A huge hiccup, if you will, is that at the end of March I contracted COVID! I spent several days in ICU, developed double pneumonia and then my liver went septic. Moreover, doctors and nurses were consumed with saving my life, but this time it was like a Halloween nightmare. I was not allowed visitors, every person who entered my room had to be gowned and gloved up; I felt so alone and isolated. This was probably my second scariest health scare. I almost died, not by my own hands, but God had different plans for me. He told me to pick up my mat and get walking again. My latest caregiver was so frightened when I almost died in her arms that she quit. The system wasn't equipped to help me quickly, so recovery was much slower than I would have liked. God had something else in mind, and I hired my first male caregiver. He was so gregarious, generous and a perfect gentleman in every way. I think everyone in my life was surprised, but he just fit right into my new life so perfectly and was my final caregiver. Greg and I have so many memories, and our lives will forever be intertwined. When I went home recently to visit friends and family, Greg was included. He is seen, not only by me but by everyone, as a member of my amazing Tribe.

In July of 2022, I finally reached 100 pounds lost. I tried on a size 18 pair of pants, and they fit. Incredible, as I hadn't fit into anything under a size 20 in 20 plus years. Knee replacement was officially scheduled for October! Miracles do happen. My weight loss was totally visible now, and it was difficult for me emotionally. Satan wanted me to believe that others only cared because I looked better on the outside. I felt fragile and emotional and tried to get a grip on it. But some days I felt like I was drowning and found myself wanting to retreat. I remember listening to a song from Beyoncé that talked about feeling like a train wreck or a puzzle with missing pieces. The song spoke of desiring to be authentically loved, flaws and all. This was my heart, and it is still my heart today. I simply want to be loved and see potential in my flaws.

By the 17th of November, I had the first of two surgeries to replace my bone-grinding-on-bone knees. I had officially reached 220 pounds and was 10% from my ultimate goal of being 200 or less. Left Total Knee Replacement, or LTKR, surgery was so much more painful and difficult than I ever could have imagined. Bone pain is intense, and all the therapy and physical needs have made it clear to me that, even one year prior, I couldn't have done this recovery without the weight loss and new health I was currently enjoying. This is another opportunity to share about learning to be your own best advocate, especially within healthcare. I have never had a good or easy reaction to new meds but especially to pain medication.

Opioids are addictive, come with a long list of side effects and should never be taken lightly. My team and I did a ton of research as I always want to do what's best for my liver, and medications are more often than not processed through the liver. In Washington state, marijuana or THC is legal, and when combined with CBD is often used to treat nausea, chronic pain and anxiety. I wanted to try this form of medication, because I found it less harmful for my liver. As a bonus, it took the edge off of the common stresses associated with surgical pain. We created a medical log, planned appropriate times and doses and successfully used it throughout my recovery. I made choices throughout my care that, although non-traditional, worked best for me. When traditional medicine was not working for me, I decided to think outside the box and do research on alternative methods. I didn't just accept what the doctor was telling me. Asking those questions and doing that research helped me come to a solution that worked in my best interests.

By December, I was hovering between 207-210 consistently and had started working out in the pool at the gym. Water has been my happy, safe space for much of my life, so I chose to start there. Through the writing process, memories are activated, and I feel led to share at this juncture an important part of my journey which happened when I was young. What little I remember and was shared with me about my life before adoption was filled with some pretty dark terrors, and one of them involved water. Apparently, an uncle of mine was pretty abusive; he and his sons found it fun to throw me in the deep end of a pool. Wait until I almost drowned and then pull me out. Not sure about you, but I do not find this humorous. As you can imagine, it was pretty traumatic for a toddler. When my adoptive mother later tried to put me in a bathtub, bring me near a pool or any large body of water, I would scream and cry. She finally managed to get me comfortable with bathtime, but other water was something I continued to be frightened of.

Southern California was a place where many social functions took place at or near the waterfront. Pool parties were a standard, and surfing was one of the coolest things you could do. My older brothers were surfers and would have loved for me to join them. Best friends wanted me to splash in the pool with them for their birthday, but I simply could not. One day, at about the age of nine, I was walking home from school when I passed a gate with a sign posted for swimming lessons. I scribbled the telephone number onto my hand before I could change my mind and ran home to beg my mom for lessons. I am truly not sure what triggered this, but I am eternally happy that I didn't chicken out. My mother, after her shock subsided, called and scheduled my lessons. The woman who coached me was so gentle, patient and helpful that in no time at all, I was swimming confidently. My favorite part of the experience was learning to float. To let my body be held up by the water. I found it soothing and healing in a way which is hard to describe. Next came the ocean. You can't see the bottom, and there are other things like seaweed, shells and fish - even sharks in there. You also have to contend with undercurrents, riptides and other natural forces within the water. It didn't happen overnight, but I kept at it and found my new happy safe space. I loved hanging off the end of a surfboard, and the beach became my favorite place on the entire planet. To this day, I can close my eyes with no fear, smell the salt in the air, hear the seagulls and feel the gritty sand on my skin and in my hair. It is a little slice of heaven. I mention all this so you know that despite your fears, you can overcome and learn to love something you were once afraid of.

Subsequently, it was natural for me to embrace my need for exercise in a pool. I started with lots of aquatic exercises (water walking, jogging and treading water) and about five laps, which quickly progressed to ten laps. On dry land, I could slowly walk up and down three flights of stairs and was consistently walking 5K steps a day! In the new year, by the end of January, I was hovering at 201 and having huge victories in and out of the pool. There was a time I found myself alone in the pool area with six men. I didn't panic; I kept swimming and simply ignored them all.

It took me until April to break my final barrier and was now 198 pounds! My Bariatric Team has given me high fives and called me a Rock Star. By the end of April I was down to 195, which is 160 pounds lost for those counting along with me! I do want to make another important point here. My journey of weight loss is mine and not yours. I mention the numbers only so you can have a clear picture of my physical transformation, but for me it has never been about the numbers. This goes for the scale, what you put into your body and how society measures us. The goal for me became about self-esteem and self-worth which can never be measured by a scale or another person. We do not gain or lose weight because we ate 300 calories of yogurt versus 300 calories of pasta and meatballs. Rather, when we seek balance, we become mindfully aware of what is coming into our bodies and find peace with the amazing creations we are; instead of losing weight or being tied to a scale; we are transformed inside and out.

I was committed to a daily routine, instituted sleep hygiene, was focused on photography, writing, music and all things which might bring me joy or help me give God all the glory. I began engaging with my church's singles ministry, going out to theater, movies, wine tastings, parks and concerts. My grandlittles loved that I could now get on their level for story time, jump on a trampoline or push them for hours in a swing. I chose to start my own podcast, entered photo contests and even read poetry for a local radio station. I have even been able to have my driver's license reinstated! I was finally living the rich and full life that God had desired for me. Pretty awesome and incredible. Overall, my health continues to improve; my energy levels are way up. My liver, on the other hand, has not improved and is beginning to store up iron while it continues to decline slowly. I am working with specialists and will have to wait and see about a liver transplant, then further what God has in mind for me next. Life is everything I could never have imagined. Peace, trust, and love are all abounding, and my confidence levels are on the rise.

Today I remain between 192-198 and am extremely happy. Yes, according to the world I am still overweight, but this was never about the numbers. For me, it was about learning to love myself and the beautiful creation I am in my Father's love. I chose to have 14 pounds of skin removed, which came with more risks and emotional triggers, but I continue taking life one day at a time. Skin removal is not for everyone and is a very personal choice. Due to limited insurance, I was only able to have the skin removed from my abdomen, as the rest is considered truly cosmetic. I am so happy with my choice.

As I close this bariatric section out, I believe it is once again important to mention the people and the positives of this experience. My sons continue to be my biggest cheerleaders, and we remain close despite the fact that they have both started their own families and have significant others. I have heard it said that trauma and tragedy either pull you apart or draw you closer, and I am thankful my sons and I fall under the latter classification. Several of my best friends are counselors - not mine, but none of them are above lending me sound advice and being the most unconditionally loving friends anyone could ask for. As my vulnerability and transparency continue to grow, so does my willingness to trust. This has brought many new friendships and people I know I can count on. Within the healthcare and social services systems, I have created the most amazing relationships with a team of professionals who are invested in me and my healthy journey. We are our own best advocates, but even more, we need to be actively involved in our care. I do lots of research, ask tons of questions and never hesitate to speak up if I think my care is not top-notch. I have finally figured out that my body and I deserve the very best, and I will fight for it, if necessary. I have also learned to utilize social media, listen to podcasts, and I pretty much read anything I can get my hands on (definitely non-fiction but pleasure as well).

We need so much input, and it need not only be educational. I am learning to laugh more, find joy in some of the smallest moments and use my God-given talents for more than just hobbies. I have written two children's books and one Christian inspirational memoir. I have helped several authors self-publish their own books. I am beginning to take my photography to the next level and have even had some of my pictures in virtual galleries. I am happily using my event coordinating skills with friends and family, as well as bringing in a modest income as a life-coach. My hope and prayer is, as my health continues to improve, I will be able to use all these gifts and talents to make enough to stop depending on disability. I am looking into things like what it might entail to live at least part-time in another part of the country or overseas.

The future is so full of possibilities, and the sky is truly the limit. I mentioned previously I had an opportunity to share poetry on a local radio broadcast and wanted to share with you a poem I was inspired to write in response. The show was called Poetry Moments, and we were asked to read aloud from our favorite poets or share something we had written. I believe a writer's desire is to present artful, yet appropriate, words which make a lovely foundation and is only the beginning of the writer's and reader's symbiotic journey. Acquainting the reader with new ideas, helping others acquire knowledge and often attesting to harsh realities are considered relevant - as is attempting to lighten the mood with laughter and hope. Atonement is considered apropos, yet aspirations are only fulfilled for both parties once the words have been written and read. As a writer, my greatest desire has been to help myself and others to not only Carpe Diem but to Carpe Spero, so let's Seize Hope together!

Hospitals, before surgeries

Transformed, inside and out

I Am Enough by Lori Leigh

If our bodies keep the score
Than mine is up for MVP
Not for how I look or
Even what I contribute to society.
Not for my brains or talents
Or how well I perform for others.
Not even for my black belt in
Overcoming trauma, abuse, neglect
And all the obstacles life has thrown at me.
Simply because I was created -
Miraculously made.
I was created to live, laugh, love
Through my faith
I can bring Glory, Honor and Praise
To an otherwise feeble and pointless existence.
I don't need to compete with false
Images, ideas and insecurities.
I no longer need to be "BIG" to be strong.
I am not weak because I am small.
It's My Life!
I am no longer waiting for a magical future
In which I must be perfect enough to succeed in.
I value the Spirit which animates my body.
In My creation I have found value.
I Am Enough!

---

[32] Hershkovich, L. (2023, May 14). *Stand strong, firm and rooted like a solid tree. Though distractions may cause you to waiver…*

"That person is like a tree planted by streams of water, which yields its fruit in season and whose leaf does not wither-whatever they do prosper."
Psalm 1:3 NIV

Chapter Eleven

I have found that the darker the clouds, the more profoundly beautiful are the silver linings. Thus, I wanted to share a very personal silver lining from my otherwise dark past and felt this would be a great opportunity. My grandmothers were two of the most instrumental women in my life. Mimi and Mamo, daughter and mother, and, in my opinion, best friends. Growing up and watching their relationship always made me wonder what happened between my mother and myself. It's not that their relationship was perfect. It was simply that they worked at and determined that their relationship would be workable/good no matter what. There was investment and a sense of unconditional love for one another, and I was loved that same way. I cherished every moment with them, and I know they are a huge part of my living legacy. My hope and prayer is that I am that loving and instrumental within my own grandchildren's lives.

My grandmothers were oil painters, amazing cooks, journalers, the hostesses with the mostest. They watched Jeopardy! and Wheel of Fortune, played solitaire late into the evening and watched Johnny Carson before finally settling down to sleep. Because of this, they slept in late. I don't think either of them started their day before ten AM. If you drove past and the curtains were still drawn it was your signal they weren't ready for company. Mamo loved to garden, and her roses were a great sense of pride for her, and Mimi loved to listen to baseball on the Radio. When the Olympics came around, we watched every sport possible. We made scrapbooks with our favorite athletes and sports and followed every amazing moment. Mimi was often our stand-in parent, as my mother was in her third marriage and she and dad traveled a lot. I remember one year we even began our new school year with Mimi, because mom and dad were off traveling.

One of my favorite memories was from that time. Every year before school, we basically received a new wardrobe. Because we were with Mimi, it turned into a fashion show. We wrote out 3x5 cards with the details of each piece of clothing worn by my sister and myself, and we took turns walking down the makeshift catwalk dressed in our new school finery. Music, pretend microphones and so much laughter. I remember another time spent with Mimi. We created a zoo with all our stuffed animals. I mentioned earlier that the kitchen was a place I ran away from, but not when my grandmothers were around.

They seemed to be able to tame my mother's temper, and the kitchen was transformed into a magical place. Maybe this is why I love the holidays so much, because my grandmothers were always there in the kitchen, patiently teaching me to make gravy, cookies, turkey and cakes. The table was always so beautifully perfect. Each glass was placed with care, and everyone was welcome and had a place at a table set by my grandmothers. My grandmother's gatherings and parties were so fun and everyone coveted an invitation.

Now that I think of it, it's definitely a huge part of why I spent most of my life in the hospitality industry. It was such a connecting part of my life where love and laughter thrived in my memories and the events I was inspired to create. A true part of my living legacy and an arena in which I truly thrived and blossomed. To this day, the few things I know how to cook came from them, and, if you know me, this is a huge accomplishment as I can burn water. So, cooking from scratch is for others much more talented than myself. But I can take something from a box and make it look gourmet. This, too, is a skill. My grandmothers were definitely a silver lining in my otherwise dark existence.

The unlikely angels in disguise are another of my silver linings: doctors, nurses, professors, co-workers, social workers, sisters and brothers in the faith, and some of the most amazing friends a person could ever hope for. It is difficult to explain how these angels impacted my life and that of my sons later in life. Yes, sometimes it was financially, but more often than not it was simply a listening ear, an empathetic heart, a shared meal or a cup of coffee, gifts and school supplies, wrestling shoes, tutors and mentors. My sons were surrounded by a village who truly took care of their every need and even their desires. As a single mother, I did avail myself of grants, scholarships, food stamps, state medical, and, if I thought my sons might benefit, I learned to be humble and ask - more times than I can count the answer was, "Yes I can help you". I have folks in my life who have tried to make me feel bad for living like this; in my eyes - and based on scriptures - we were given a share-the-wealth card. Just like in the game of LIFE, in real life, when we have, we are to share wealth. When we don't have, someone shares it with us. If we don't have the money, we can volunteer and give of all our gifts and talents. I have never been big on making money from garage sales. I usually donate or give to a friend in need. I have found that in so doing, whenever a need has arisen, God has supplied through an organization or friend. Reciprocal love in action.

Throughout this time, many miracles happened, and I desire to share a few with you. As I mentioned earlier, many of my professors have become my lifelong friends. I was recently reunited with one, and his part in my amazing journey was brought back to life. His father was actually my professor, and I attribute much of my maturity in my writing and life skills to him. However, when the Bubbs came into my life, I was struggling with my new life-altering, liver diagnosis and having issues with my state medical. Dan suggested a shot in the dark. He was going to write to President Obama and see if I could get the help I needed to get my medical insurance reinstated. I agreed, but I don't think either of us really expected a response - definitely not the miraculous call from the head of Medicaid or the subsequent letter I personally received from the Obama administration. Needless to say, my Medicaid was immediately reinstated, and I have never had an issue with it since. Another similar story from that year was with a lovely woman I became friends with while at Gonzaga. Sue was a student faculty advisor, but in reality, she is an angel in disguise. While she was on a mission trip with Desmond Tutu, she just happened to mention me. Next thing I know, I was on the prayer list of a Cardinal. Lest you think it was only professors who were angels walking in my life... fast forward a few years to right after my stroke. I was fully engaged in every kind of therapy (physical, occupational and speech). My recovery was moving forward nicely, but my home situation was proving difficult. I was living with my youngest son and his girlfriend at the time, and it was up three flights of stairs. As you can imagine, this was not possible for me yet and proving difficult for getting released from the hospital. A lovely couple approached me and casually mentioned they knew I was in need and asked if they would be able to help in any way. I asked for prayers and was prepared to let it go at that. They had something much more tangible in mind. They wanted to purchase me a handicap accessible home. Excuse me? And they would hold it in trust for me so as not to affect my disability and tiny income. As you can imagine, my sons and I were incredulous and overwhelmed with the love and commitment of these beautiful friends. God can, and will, meet your every need and desire if you just let Him. I lived in my God-provided-for home until the next amazing season of life. Cliff hangers are great...right? I promise I won't leave you hanging for too long.

As soon as a young giant sequoia has an adequate year-round supply of moisture and sunlight, it begins to grow quite rapidly. Under optimal conditions, its main stem leads the way upward, and the tree becomes conical in shape. Once giant sequoias have germinated and developed into strong young seedlings with good root systems, they are quite capable of surviving in many parts of the world.[33]

Theoretically, it would appear that a giant sequoia could go on living and growing forever. Death comes to them only by means of fire or through some other external physical event such as undermining by erosion or overthrow by the wind. Although they are no longer considered the oldest living things in the world, they could conceivably regain the title at some time in the future. Today, the oldest known giant sequoia is some 3,200 years of age.[34]

Excerpt from *The Enduring Giants* by Joseph H. Engbeck Jr., published by the California State Parks.

Just like my Sequoia, I had to take root and branch out, and although it took me a while to do so, that is exactly what I have done. I am rooted in my faith, in the love of family and friends, in a strong desire to love myself and others through the richest, fullest life I can. My perseverance is my enduring nature, so I may live longer and stronger than anyone thought possible. God continues to reveal new branches through numerous

> opportunities to serve the community and environment I am surrounded with. I seem, like my Sequoia, to be able to live just about anywhere with almost anyone in any environment, whether hostile or loving, and not only survive but thrive. I chose Carpe Spero (Seize Hope). Rather than just a day, I desire to seize eternity! [35]

I would like to share one more of my poems with you as we close out. I do not consider myself a poet but one who dabbles. Poetry has always been a huge part of my life and a way for me to process my feelings and emotions. It's where I find passion, encouragement and hope. The power of the written word is made even more beautiful when read aloud, so I encourage you to do that with this poem and any others you may come across. I thank you all for helping me through this book and my writings to leave a Living Legacy.

With my grandmothers

Rocking Chairs by Lori Leigh

When you are eighty and seated on the porch
With your best friend,
In your sought-after matching,
But comfortable rocking chairs,
Time can appear to be the Vampire.
But the time for fear should be long past.
In the days spent raising children,
Laughing in the kitchen
Or crying together while watching your favorite movie.
There will be no need for fears or regrets
If you shared your favorite books,
Savored long walks together on sandy beaches
And fondly remember
Teasing one another mercilessly.
Then there is no reason to fear
The Valkyrie soon coming
If we all must sleep eternally
Than what better way to prepare ourselves
Than gently rocking on the porch
With your best friend.
All the while the seeds of your friendship blossom
As your life's blood enriches the soil
With the final kiss from the Vampire of Time
Not only to grace you as you slip into eternal rest
But by the lives of all those
You chanced to touch.

[33] Engbeck, J. H., Jr. (1988). *The enduring giants.* California State Parks.
[34] National Park Service. (n.d.). *Sequoia research*. Yosemite National Park. https://www.nps.gov/yose/learn/nature/sequoia-research.htm
[35] Engbeck, J. H., Jr. (1988). *The enduring giants.* California State Parks.

"Blessed is the one who trusts in the Lord, whose confidence is in him. They will be like a tree planted by the water that sends out its roots by the stream. It does not fear when heat comes; its leaves are always green. It has no worries in a year of drought and never fails to bear fruit."

Jeremiah 17:7-8

Chapter Twelve

I can't tell you how many times I get asked, but how did you do it? How did you survive? What's the Secret to living richly and fully? Where do your strength and tenacity come from, your survival instincts? What does it take to almost break someone so ambitious and competitive? If my life is a testament to the strength of the human spirit, then I desire to formulate and model for others through the power of the written word. I believe our enemy is prowling back and forth and constantly desiring for us to falter, but it is not one thing, one event, one trauma. It is against something supernatural, and this enemy will go to great lengths to see us fail.

However, even more important to grasp is how far God will go to bring us back. In my writer's group I was recently sharing with my friends that my grandmothers and mother all journaled, and this is one of the greatest pieces of my legacy. What I learned through reading their words is that my grandmothers more or less cataloged their daily activities and briefly shared some joys and losses. Looking back at my mother's words, I could see all the masks she was still wearing even while journaling. Upon further discovery, the first half of my life or a little more, I was wearing those masks and many more. I wasn't able to be free with my words, out of preservation or fear of rejection or simply unable to face the truth. In the past decade, especially in the last five years, I have finally taken off the masks, become transparent and completely vulnerable. Through counseling, a stronger relationship with my Creator and through the unconditional love of my Tribe, I have finally been able to be uninhibited within my journals. It's been powerful and transformational, combing through some of my personal diaries and writings. I thought this might be the best way to help others grasp how I not only survived but completely overcame and triumphed in my personal and professional life. I am going to share random snippets and stories from my journals in hopes that we can Carpe Spero together.

15 Mar

Wow! Satan seems to be working overtime, and my mental and emotional plates are beyond full. My own recent brush with death, the passing of my brother, Little Bobby, resulted in a glimpse back into the Game of Thrones that is my family - the anger, stark fear, need for control and power. Makes me want to run away again...thank goodness I don't have to. Alex is facing job changes which are undesirable and causing daily angst, thus me as we are living together. Changes and failures in my current caregiving agency. The normal ebb and flow within the lives of my friends and loved ones. Then all you can do is laugh when the toilet breaks-really God! If I didn't have God's love, grace and mercy, I would seriously need to be committed to the local psych ward. Thank Goodness tomorrow is a new day...

3 April

Why is it we hear little of life not going as planned? I need to know how real life collides with Faith. I think if I am honest with myself, fear is at the center. Fear of not being accepted in my imperfection. Fear of failing. Fear of not being enough for my loved ones, friends, let alone myself. I desire to learn how to trust my unknowns to God, more than I trust my ability to control. I want to trust Him more than any outcome or plan. Can I learn how to have an expectant posture with my Father? Or do I keep trusting in a 12-step program, self-help book etc...I want and need to throw my hands up and Let Jesus Work! Let Him weave my passions, pains, joys and tears as only He can within His Master Plans. I want to do life with my Savior! I am relinquishing my feeble attempts, my need for control, my people pleasing goals. I am taking off the masks I have painstakingly created and worn for almost a half a century. I am realizing that although the masks have served some good purposes-protection, energy, flexibility and fun-in the end they were actually stifling and smothering me. With masks, I could never truly be free. Only with God's love can I truly transition healthily into all that God has in mind for me. His visions are so much grander than mine, more fulfilling and perfect! The masks, presuppose a false perfection when my Father wants to be beautifully revealed in the mess. All so that His unconditional love, grace and mercy can not only be revealed but shine in all His Glory!

1 May

As another year is passing and I will be one year older, I desire to ask myself some of the hard questions. Am I sacrificing my sanity, family or health to make some project or event happen? Will I or my loved ones not be better served by my taking a nap, getting much needed rest or simply learning to be still? And most importantly am I still finding joy in sharing my gifts and talents? Am I enjoying the journey? I read the words, sing the songs, smile, serve and pour myself into all things church and loving others. I am exhausted! I am slowly realizing that I have been mistaking intimacy with my Heavenly Father with responsibility. As if life is one long party/event, I was in charge of coordinating. Seeking flawless perfection! Ignoring complications, bowling over obstacles and being reckless with my health, my temple. My loving Father is whispering to me...no daughter, your unrealistic expectations for perfection aren't real. My Creator loves spontaneity, the unexpected, so why can't I? I will continue to fail and be discouraged if my hope is based on my education, my skills, or my will. I need to figure out how to tap into the powerful manifestation of the Holy Spirit. I desire a heart ready for joy and pain, dancing and resting, and a heart ready for every experience under the sun. I am seeking authenticity, vulnerability, and transparency. I want to push out the need to perfectly orchestrate each moment and simply be...My life or at least the rest of it, is going to be a Leap of Faith! Geronimo!

16 July

Although somewhere deep down in my heart I know God is my creator, even more difficult for me to grasp is that He wants to have a relationship with little ol me. Maybe if I could just get comfortable with this idea, then the insatiable hunger and loneliness could be finally met or rather fulfilled. Until I grasp onto or wait...simply BE STILL! Simply get to know my Heavenly Father. Until I get these concepts, I will still be powerless, filled with anxiety and continue to please others rather than my Father. But it's a new day! As I reflect on the Lord's Glory, I can be transformed into His likeness. I can be renewed like an eagle, refreshed through the Spirit. I can be transparent and live from the inside out. Although I have been hurt, I know that my God's love will always find me. God, Your love is freeing me, it's freeing my soul. Slowly, my dreams are free. When I stop to look up instead of wandering lost in the storms of this life, I can face all my fears. I can be confident in God's goodness if I will stop running in the sinking sands of this desolate world. It is indeed a NEW DAY!

23 July

Early mornings are not easy for me, but I can after my morning meds, give my first part of my day to commune with my Creator. It is necessary to draw close to my Father so that I can withstand the pressures and challenges which will inevitably hit me today. To stave off the scrutiny of my unrelenting critics, especially those inner critics which are living rent free in my mind. I really need to examine how to kick them out. As I jealously guard my time with my Father then I can have poise, be boldly courageous, show compassion, have patience - unending reserves only come from a closeness with God. No more excuses, girl. Logic as well as life experience indicates the importance of morning prayer and the study of the Word so get to it...

25 Aug

While reading the Beauty of Broken I was reminded that my layers of loss, trauma and brokenness can be displayed as a beautiful tapestry. Especially when viewed through the lens of humility, courage, faith, love, respect, forgiveness, and thankfulness. My life can be REDEEMED! *I want to lose the desperation with which I have been approaching things lately. I desire to attach myself to God, not perfection, not works, not my family, especially not this world which is not my home. I want to sit with my brokenness in all its imperfections so that I can be reformed into something beautiful; someone loved unconditionally and somehow useful in my brokenness. I have heard it said that without experiencing pain, it is difficult to truly experience joy. Through my pain, I can let what looks to be holes in my life be places filled with hope! God is trying to get me to work out my bitterness-to allow grace to propel me to new heights. He wants to ease my pain through confronting my grief and disappointment. He desires me to relinquish any need for self-righteousness. Only then can I know serenity. When I quit all that is damaging to my soul and invest in truth, responsibility and humility I can face reality and enjoy true freedom. My sackcloth is replaced with glorious garments. My wounds are healed and truth becomes my shield. Walking in light, my paths are made straight, my soul is no longer downcast. My broken life can be a display of God's Glory because my Creator and the Spirit fill me with a peace that passes this world's understanding.*

Undated & Random Thoughts from Lori

- *Authenticity is a synonym for Jesus…*
- *When I come across people, I can sometimes see an empty shell. I wonder what happened to them. When they were presented with a Crossroad and given the opportunity to turn left or right, why did they choose neither? Triggers, trauma, fear, anxiety... I personally am sick of being timid, afraid or consumed with what someone else thinks or feels I should choose.*
- *I want more than mountain top experiences. I want to love and embrace the simplest moments, especially when Jesus is there with me in the small steps.*
- *Because we can't find something, it doesn't mean it doesn't exist. If love and family are who we choose then embrace whichever community celebrates with you and embraces you. Choose your Tribe!*
- *My faith was performance-based. I used God like a seasonal accessory. I invited Him into my life for the Big Party's, hoping He would simply provide my just desserts. Never realizing my Father preferred my quiet times-usually a cup of coffee, a simple meal, some laughter and even some tears-every breath in and out.*
- *True Faith doesn't listen to the voice of fear. Faith focuses on what we don't see, but fear focuses on what we see. Faith is a conscious choice to believe that my God is in every situation no matter the circumstances. My faith assures me that life will go on...and before I know it, I am smiling again. Thomas Aquinas said it best, "to one who has faith no explanation is necessary, to one without faith no explanation is possible."*
- *The more impossible it seems, the greater the love is!*

- *There is Hope for all of us even the most broken of souls.*
- *Just like Tina Turner, I came of age later in my life and that's okay…*
- *We have to realize that some of the worst parts of our story are what's inspiring. There is something unique and powerful about my story.*
- *We can't let pain have the whole conversation, especially if the best rewards are only revealed in the mindful examination of the whole journey.*

One of my many times journaling with a great drink

"Trees are as close to immortality as the rest of us ever come."
Karen Joy Fowler [36]

Epilogue

There are days when writing is difficult. Especially when loss, conflict and general everyday drama is on overdrive. A friend suggested I write through it, but wow, this has truly been a difficult task.

While watching a show recently, a line stuck out: "This was almost a good night." So, what exactly constitutes a good night? Is it the meal, fellowship or simply just downtime? Maybe it's a good show or a sporting event? Maybe it's snuggling in a warm blanket, going to bed early or late, whichever motivates you - or maybe it's none of the above. For me tonight, a good night has been a combination of things: a decent meal, a glass of wine, watching an old, familiar show while typing, all the while wrapped up in a cozy blanket and sitting on the edge of my bed. Honestly, I'm trying to shut out the noise and just be in my own space. Texting a friend and praying have also made the list.

No longer do triggers destroy or distract for too long my plans for a rich, full life. For example, as I was writing this book, my sister-in-law sent me a batch of old pictures. Previously, looking through all those old memories, I might have been triggered or put on edge. Today, I love that in my growth and mindfulness I can simply find reasons to laugh or find silver linings within these previously tumultuous memories.

I am blessed to be able to enjoy special time with my sons, and my momma's heart is on cloud nine. As they have grown up and begun their own families, mom moments are few and far between. So, when they occur, I embrace them fully and try to capture each feeling, each tear, each bout of laughter so I can treasure them into the next life.

As a new year is quickly approaching, for the first time in several decades, I am truly hopeful and excited to see what new adventures God and I will have over this next season. I have some trips planned. The grandlittles, numbering six now, will be playing sports, dancing, having adventures with friends and a myriad of things within their classrooms and with their families. I am blessed to have easy access to all of it. Being a grandmother is honestly the greatest blessing one can never imagine until it is upon you. I continue helping to shepherd our singles ministry, and I'm always looking for new opportunities to serve in God's Kingdom.

I am working with a best friend and sister of my heart. We established our own company to help others self-publish and share their own stories. At this moment, Rainy Day Self-Publishing LLC has almost ten clients and more on the way. We are a bit of a geek family, so Dungeons & Dragons (D&D) will definitely play a part in our gatherings. Concerts, plays, the symphony and whatever else I am able to engage in will definitely remain a priority as I want to fully engage in life. Building relationships and legacy and all these things assist with that.

Lastly, I want to also take some time to address another area within my transformational journey which has occurred. More often than not when we let something go, God, fate, the universe, finds a way to give us what our heart desires, even if we don't know of the desire. A couple years ago, I attended my second singles conference. I mention that it's my second, because as I have previously noted for my first one, I was fully engaged as Martha. If you are wondering who Martha is, she is a wonderful example of a servant in God's Word. However, she found herself tired and in need of assistance. She even boldly approached Jesus to see if He would get her sister, Mary, to help her. Jesus explained to Martha that her sister was exactly where she needed to be. I am not a Biblical scholar, but my humble interpretation of this story is not that Martha was wrong but perhaps not focusing on her relationship with Jesus. Mary was sitting at the feet of Jesus, in that moment, exactly where she needed to be. My previous experience within the hospitality industry often lands me in an organizational role when it comes to events, especially within my Kingdom Family. So, although I was praised for my first singles conference and its huge success, I personally didn't get to participate very much. In my journaling and processing after this first experience, I realized I had a desire to enjoy a singles conference as an attendee and not the organizer. I found a conference down in San Diego, and before I could chicken out, I bought my ticket, arranged for travel and sat on my hands every time we were asked to volunteer. I was determined this time to be more like Mary and to sit at the feet of teachers, enjoy fellowship, and take in every new opportunity.

It is important to make note that on this journey down to the conference, this book was conceived. I was sharing some of my story with the sisters who were with me, and we chose to make a pit stop in the Redwood National Forest. We took pictures, and I literally hugged a tree and laughed so hard I almost peed my pants. The subsequent journeys to and from this singles conference remain in my mind and heart as important as the conference itself.

Although I am an extrovert, I found myself overwhelmed on the first evening. I knew only a few people there; the music was fantastic. If a bit loud, there were throngs of strangers, and I felt I had no real purpose. How do you Marys do it? I felt like a fish out of water with no real direction. I slowly settled in and began to engage in my well-known social skills. Throughout the weekend, there were amazing speakers, sumptuous food choices, the beach (my ultimate happy space), and I met so many wonderful new folks. One, in particular, was a man just a few years my senior, with a beautiful voice, sweet smile and such an amazing heart for God and others. I did not go to this conference looking for anyone but God somehow managed to slip one person in particular, under the radar. We went on a fun encouragement date Saturday, then Sunday were thrown together once again. I had the great pleasure of hitching a ride to Vegas with him and a young man he was mentoring. I was blessed to meet his youngest daughter, a lovely young UNLV student, majoring in English and desiring to break into the publishing world.

God is so Great, and I love divine meetings. I honestly am not sure why, but this man and I continued to text even after returning home. We decided to have a Zoom date with another couple, and it went amazingly well. So, we decided to meet weekly via technology and see where this new relationship just might be going. We were able to meet up face-to-face, Super Bowl Weekend. I met some of his family, we enjoyed some amazing fellowship, and I learned that Bingo at the Elks Lodge in a small town is a serious matter. All joking aside, we decided maybe our families should meet up, and we have had a few of these family gatherings now. Both our adult kids have taken the time and effort to engage with us, as well with one another. We laugh, talk, immerse ourselves in tourist stuff and simply enjoy time together. It's been an amazing whirlwind which has left me desiring more. You have read my story above, and you know trust, vulnerability and men, in particular, are something I have struggled with my whole life. To say this new relationship and my desire for it to continue is from way out in left field is not farfetched, yet every call, text, date and time together leaves me with peace and a strong desire for more. I am constantly asking God what He is doing to me? Could Cinderella find her happily ever after? Can this broken woman find peace and contentment with another? I believe the answer is yes!

As a strong, independent woman I also feel it is important to point out that I do not believe we need to be rescued or completed with a partner. Ever After and Pretty Woman are two Cinderella examples for me which stick out to this day as strong women who chose to love and be loved in return. Biblically speaking, Esther and Ruth are my heroines, and I encourage you to take some time and read their stories of Courage and Redemption. We are not promised tomorrow, so God asks us to take each day as it comes, and that is what I am doing. I said, "YES!" to the ring, to the dress, to the whole new world! I am no longer a victim, a survivor or even an overcomer. I am a transformed, beautiful new creation who is seeking to Seize Hope wherever it may be found. I am a Sequoia, planted by a stream, ready to give all the Glory to her Creator. Let's Carpe Spero together.

My Prince Charming

---

36 Fowler, K. J. (2004). *The Jane Austen book club*. G. P. Putnam's Sons.

Resources

If you or anyone you know is suffering from mental health issues, eating disorders, domestic violence and abuse, or anything else, there is help!

NEDA Helpline Support for individuals and families affected by eating disorders. Phone: 1-800-931-2237 Text: 741741 Website: https://www.nationaleatingdisorders.org/

National Domestic Violence Hotline Support, crisis intervention, and safety planning for anyone affected by domestic violence. Phone: 800-799-7233 Text: 88788 Website: https://www.thehotline.org

988 Suicide & Crisis Lifeline (via NAMI) Immediate support for anyone experiencing emotional distress or a mental health crisis. Call: 988 Website: https://www.nami.org

YWCA USA Programs and support focused on eliminating racism, empowering women, and promoting community well-being. Website: https://www.ywca.org

Acknowledgements

I want to once more thank so many people who have traversed this amazing path with me. Many I have already mentioned, but I feel some need more clarification and simply more praise.

Educators are truly up for sainthood if there were such a thing. Their tireless efforts to shape, mold and form minds, young and old, is truly transformational. Ken and Dan Bubb were such an integral part of my metamorphosis and ensuing journey. Although Ken has passed away, his son, Dan, continues to encourage and support me today and every day. Ron Heiss was not only my speech and drama professor, he was also a healthy father figure for me. His mentorship and guidance are a huge part of who I am now and forevermore. Sue Weitz was one of my biggest cheerleaders throughout my time at Gonzaga. Suzanne Ostersmith was a part of my wonderful experience at Gonzaga as well. Through a class called Movement In Theater, secretly it was a dance class, I was totally unprepared for, LOL! However, her class was also an opportunity to hone my journaling skills, push myself in every way, physically, mentally and spiritually. She also took a huge chance with me in my first major acting role as her narrator in The Crane Wife. Stacy Kowtko remains, to this day, one of my best friends. She challenged me intellectually, politically and helped my love of history and people grow exponentially. I am blessed that I am still able to call her and so many other professors, friends and colleagues. Good schools don't only have excellent teachers and professors, they have loving and compassionate employees in financial aid, admissions, hospitality, advisory boards, groundskeepers and janitorial staff. A good educational system is like an extended family.

Caregivers within the system, and without it, are truly angels in disguise. Doctors who listen, care and choose to have good bedside manners are so appreciated. Nurses and CNA's definitely don't get enough recognition. They are the heartbeat of your care inside and out of the hospital. The individual caregivers who I have had the honor of taking care of me are almost too numerous to recount, but I will attempt. Sara, Leila, Nadia, EJ, and Greg are just a few names which come to mind. They have all been a huge part of my story and have helped me to create a living legacy. Physical Therapists, Occupational Therapists, Speech Therapists, Surgeons, Endocrinologists, Gastroenterologists, Cardiologists, Nutritionists and Mental Health experts all make up a part of a good Care Team and are essential for our survival and long-term wellbeing. I cannot thank them enough for being a part of my Tribe.

Pastors, Leaders in the Church, Elders, Youth and Family Directors...anyone who chooses a liturgical path in this world is to be commended. They are shepherds, mentors and guides in this thing we call life, and in my humble opinion, truly called servants. The Grace, unconditional love and empathy they choose to engage in is special and needed. This is in no way meant to put them up on a pedestal, simply my way of acknowledging that my journey wouldn't have been the same without them. Pastor Schlect, Colonel Hall, Dana and Gin Perkins, Chris and Amy Schwartzenberger, Daryl and Ruby Wallace, Jacob and Lindsay Hoffman, Dallas and Jess Crockett, Phil Salvador, and simply too many others. If I have missed you, it was not intentional. I simply ask for grace and know that you have all played a roll, spiritually building me up and helping me to Carpe Spero.

Family for me is so much more than blood, it is community, it is our Tribe, those we choose to let into our inner circle. It would be impossible to name you all, but you know who you are. I tell you everyday, through calls, texts, letters and in every way I can think of. My story, my legacy would not be complete without you, and my heart is full of gratitude for your love, transparency and vulnerability with me.

My Sons and Grandchildren will always be at the center of my universe and my heart. You are each the blessing I never could have asked for or expected, and my heart is overflowing with unconditional love for each of you.

Lastly, to my beloved new Husband and his family for welcoming me into their stories, their lives and legacy. It is such a humbling opportunity that God has given to us later in life and another, truly unexpected blessing. God has given us a glimpse of eternity, and I am honored to be grasping it together.

Always and forever,

Lori Leigh

About The Author

Lori Leigh is the Co-Owner and Co-Creator of Rainy Day Self-Publishing LLC, where they encourage clients to shelve their worries for another day. The business helps others look professional while sharing their stories and creating their very own living legacy.

Lori is also a Life-Coach, Author, Editor, Photographer, and Loving Grandmother. After getting remarried, she moved from the picturesque Pacific Northwest to the scenic Southwest. She is passionate about writing, photography, and living a rich and full life. Her current favorite pastime is spending time with her six grandchildren. She is blessed to have all of her family remain close, even while separated geographically.

She also loves sports, the arts, and road trips with friends. Lori doesn't want to simply Carpe Diem, rather Carpe Spero, which is to Seize Hope. She considers herself an overcomer of childhood trauma, domestic violence, and eating disorders. She invites those around her to transform their lives, remove suffocating masks, and Seize Eternal Hope.

Signing some of my children's books

Recording for Poetry Moment, on a local radio station

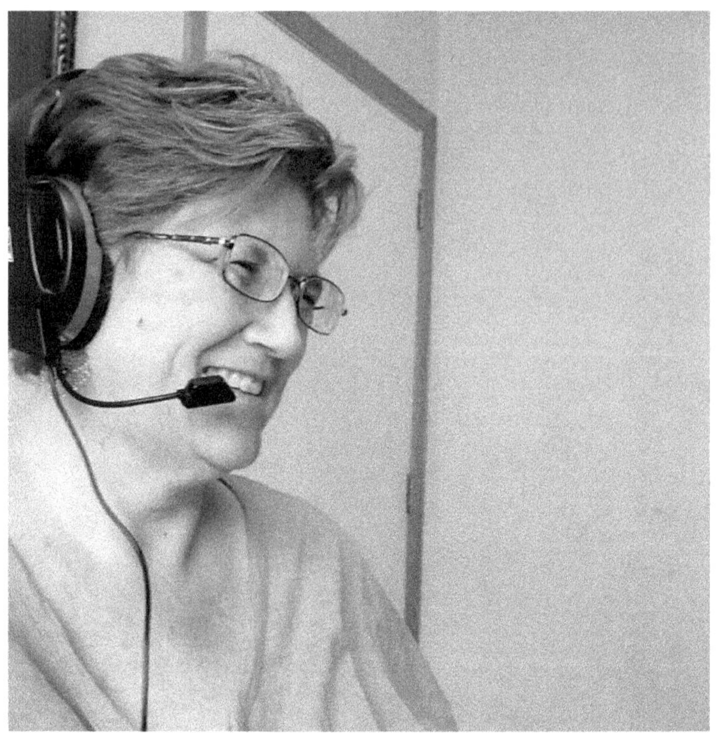

Recording Behind The Mask podcast

Logo for Behind The Mask
(You can find it on Spotify)

Also By Lori Leigh

Carpe Spero
As Rachel comes to grips with a recent diagnosis, her beloved sons David and Johnny must face their own fears as well. Their faith and family will be tested. Can light truly overpower darkness? What does it mean to leave a legacy? Is seizing hope attainable or simply an ethereal dream? Join Rachel and her sons for a brief glimpse into how they choose to Carpe Spero! Maybe someone unexpected will draw them all closer than they ever thought possible.

The Scrolls of Testimony

Have you ever watched the sunrise over the vast savannah and wondered about the animals and landscapes that call it home? Join Little Paulo Rex and his friends on an epic journey filled with discovery, adventure, and breathtaking challenges. Along the way, they celebrate family, heritage, and the hope that carries us through every high and low.

The Snow Rider

Much of Japan is covered by mountains and forests, making it a challenging place to settle. Yet in the northeastern corner lies a tiny village no human has ever discovered, waiting just for you. Explore its magic, perhaps even spotting unicorns and fairies, while adventuring in the shadows of Mt. Moiwa.

Purchases can be made on Amazon!

Lori Leigh

Rainy Day
SELF-PUBLISHING LLC

www.ingramcontent.com/pod-product-compliance
Lightning Source LLC
LaVergne TN
LVHW020635100826
845148LV00012B/2194

* 9 7 9 8 2 1 8 9 1 8 1 2 5 *